About the Author

Dr. Christopher Joseph Devine

Dr. Christopher Joseph Devine, Ph.D. is the President of Devine Guidance International, a consulting firm specializing in providing solutions for regulatory compliance, quality, supplier management, and supply-chain issues facing the medical device industry. Additionally, Dr. Devine is the author of Devine Guidance, a weekly blog focusing on the understanding of regulations mandated by the FDA and other regulatory bodies; and published by the Medical Device Summit, an *e*-magazine. Furthermore, Dr. Devine is a member of the editorial board of the Medical Device Summit. Dr. Devine has 32-years of experience in quality assurance, regulatory affairs, and program management. He is a senior member of the American Society of Quality (ASQ), a member of Regulatory Affairs Professionals Society (RAPS), a member of the Project Management Institute (PMI) and resides on several technical advisory boards. Dr. Devine received his doctorate from Northcentral University, with his doctoral dissertation entitled, "Exploring the Effectiveness of Defensive-Receiving Inspection for Medical Device Manufacturers: A Mixed-Method Study." Dr. Devine also holds a graduate degree in organizational management (MAOM) and an undergraduate degree business management (BSBM). Prior to Dr. Devine's commercial career he served proudly as a member of the United States Marine Corps.

Dedication

To my family, especially my wife Connie, for their patience with me spending long hours on the computer; to Dr. Ron Allen, my friend and confidant, who sat on my doctoral dissertation committee, mentored me and constantly reminded me that once I received my doctorate, I was obligated to write; to Jim Twitchell and Pierre Boisier, who facilitated my pursuit of a post-graduate degree, without the support of these gentlemen, there would be no Dr. D; and finally to my parents, Joseph T. & Dorothy L. Devine, although they have passed, they would be equally proud of this accomplishment.

Acknowledgements

First and foremost, I want to thank Rick and Beth Biros and the entire staff of the Medical Device Summit. They gave me the opportunity to publish my work in a weekly forum (Devine Guidance) in this fabulous on-line industry magazine. I would also like to recognize Sangita Viswanathan, the editor of the Medical Device Summit, for her painstaking review and editing of my weekly articles.

Introduction

The purpose of Dr. D's first book is to breakdown and analyze the requirements depicted in the 21 CFR, Part 820, also known as the FDA's Quality System Regulation (QSR). The doctor tackles each of the sections sequentially and hopes the readers are able to glean some useful information while enjoying the common-sense, objective, and no-nonsense approach to complying with each of the requirements. For those of you that are frequent followers of Dr. D's weekly rants, posted in The Medical Device Summit, you will recognize the often poignant prose employed by Dr. D. That said, I really hope you enjoy the book!

Table of Contents

Chapter 1 – Devine Guidance "The Rules" 1

Chapter 2 – General Provisions 5

Chapter 3 - Management Responsibility.. 12

Chapter 4 – Quality Audits 20

Chapter 5 – Personnel 26

Chapter 6 – Design Controls 31

Chapter 7 – Document Controls 54

Chapter 8 – Purchasing Controls 61

Chapter 9 – Identification and Traceability 68

Chapter 10 – Production and Process Controls.. 76

Chapter 11 – Inspection, Measuring, and Test Equipment 104

Chapter 12 – Process Validation 116

Chapter 13 – Acceptance Activities.. 124

Chapter 14 – Nonconforming Product.. 136

Chapter 15 – Corrective and Preventive Action 144

Chapter 16 – Labeling and Packaging Control.. 153

Chapter 17 – Handling, Storage, Distribution, and Installation.. 162

Chapter 18 – Records.. 175

Chapter 19 – Servicing.. 207

Chapter 20 – Statistical Techniques.. 214

Chapter 21 – Responding to an FDA Form 483 222

Chapter 22 – Responding to an FDA Warning Letter 228

Chapter 23 – Consent Decree "Now What?".. 240

References.. 245

Chapter 1 – Devine Guidance "The Rules"

Dr. D's Rules

Ever since Dr. D's childhood, I have always had a major aversion to rules of any kind. After all, rules are established so creative folks can bend or break them. Unfortunately, bending or breaking rules in the medical device industry can result in device manufacturers ending up in regulatory purgatory or even worse. In fact, the conveyors of the rules can really unload some serious hurt on device manufacturers not willing to adhere to their rules or intentionally take liberties in regards to their rules. That said, the doctor has created a set of rules that should keep device organizations on the straight and narrow path of compliance. As you will quickly see, these rules are premised on one very simple concept, "common sense." Enjoy.

- Rule #1 - Compliance to regulations is not optional; compliance is mandatory and dictated by law.

- Rule #2 - Measuring and monitoring equipment shall be calibrated, maintained, and traceable back to a recognized standard, e.g. NIST.

- Rule #3 - Document the results of all events in writing, because if it is not documented, in writing, the event did not occur.

- Rule #4 – The FDA conducts inspections for the purpose of collecting evidence, should legal action be required; while your notified body (*remember they work for you*) conduct audits. Treat each visit accordingly.

- Rule #5 – All investigations, CAPA, Response Required SCARs, product failures, audit findings, etc. require root-cause analysis and follow-up for effectiveness of the actions pursued.

- Rule #6 – All procedures, work instructions, drawings, specifications, etc. must be written, well-documented, and controlled within a defined document control system (No napkin drawings, please).

- Rule #7 – Make sure all changes, design, process, supplier, etc. are processed through the appropriate level of verification and/or validation.

- Rule #8 – Clearly mark and segregate all non-conforming material, preferably under lock and key.

- Rule #9 – Management review is an important tool employed to gage the effectiveness of your entire organization, not just quality; so ensure all of the metrics employed to monitor your business are included into the review.

- Rule #10 – Effective design control is not an option, it is a salient requirement.

- Rule #11 – Never have your quality or regulatory organizations report into manufacturing operations, i.e., the separation of church and state rule.

- Rule #12 – Traceability is required from start to finish for everything, i.e., production, process validation, design validation, aging studies, etc.

- Rule #13 – When in doubt, read the appropriate regulation, contact your notified body, talk with your quality organization or regulatory organization, and finally yet importantly, ask for Devine Guidance.

- Rule #14 – You do not have to share the results or content of internal audits, supplier audits, or management reviews with the FDA; however, you must provide evidence that this activities are occurring.

- Rule #15 - Post-market surveillance is an important activity. Please ensure all customer complaints are actively logged, investigated to root-cause (if possible), and a response returned to the complaining organization.

- Rule #16 - Responses to MDRs should be deemed mission critical. If an organization builds a documented history of late reporting of MDRs, they can expect a visit from their friends from the agency.

Chapter 2 – General Provisions

21 CFR, Part 820

Subpart A

Chapter 2 – General Provisions

In kicking off chapter this chapter, there is really just some basic guidance Dr. D can offer. There is no special insight into the general provisions, watch outs, or super-secret translations needed for device manufacturers to comply. In fact, the crux of general provisions is really the section on agency employed definitions. That said the first piece of guidance that Dr. D can offer is for device manufacturers to become extremely fluent in the definitions delineated within the Quality System Regulations (QSR); and whenever possible, ensure continuity in your own quality management system by using terms familiar to the agency. When the agency comes for a friendly visit to your facility, and they will eventually come, using the same terminology makes the job of the FDA inspector easier. Guess what, if the agency understands how your quality management system works and it appears to be effective, your organization will not be on the receiving end of a Form 483. You can take that to the bank!

The second piece of guidance for Section 820.1 pertains to Current Good Manufacturing Practices (CGMP). Guess what, device manufactures are expected to have and sustain manufacturing environments that comply with CGMP. It is the doctor's strong opinion, complying with CGMP is part of the cost of admission to participate in the medical device industry. Call it a down payment.

The third piece of guidance offered by Dr. D pertains to the quality management system. Forget about all of the text pertaining to exemptions and variances depicted under 820.1. My best advice is to bite the bullet and implement a world-class quality management system that is fully compliant with the QSR. It is well worth the initial investment; and the FDA will be appreciative of the effort. So as Tony Soprano would say, "Forgetta bout it" only in regards to exemptions and variances, of course.

Quality System Regulation - 21 CFR, Part 820

Subpart A

820.1 Scope

(a)Applicability. (1) Current good manufacturing practice (CGMP) requirements are set forth in this quality system regulation. The requirements in this part govern the methods used in, and the facilities and controls used for, the design, manufacture, packaging, labeling, storage, installation, and servicing of all finished devices intended for human use. The requirements in this part are intended to ensure that finished devices will be safe and effective and otherwise in compliance with the Federal Food, Drug, and Cosmetic Act (the act). This part establishes basic requirements applicable to manufacturers of finished medical devices. If a manufacturer engages in only some operations subject to the requirements in this part, and not in others, that manufacturer need only comply with those requirements applicable to the operations in which it is engaged. With respect to class I devices, design controls apply only to those devices listed in 820.30(a)(2). This regulation does not apply to manufacturers of components or parts of finished devices, but such manufacturers are encouraged to use appropriate provisions of this regulation as guidance. Manufacturers of human blood and blood components are not subject to this part, but are subject to part 606 of this chapter. Manufacturers of human cells, tissues, and cellular and tissue-based products (HCT/Ps), as defined in 1271.3(d) of this chapter, that are medical devices (subject to premarket review or notification, or exempt from notification, under an application submitted under the device provisions of the act or under a biological product license application under section 351 of the Public Health Service Act) are subject to this part and are also subject to the donor-eligibility procedures set forth in part 1271 subpart C of this chapter and applicable current good tissue practice procedures in part 1271 subpart D of this chapter. In the event of a conflict between applicable regulations in part 1271 and in other parts of this chapter, the regulation specifically applicable to the device in question shall supersede the more general.

(2) The provisions of this part shall be applicable to any finished device as defined in this part, intended for human use, that is manufactured, imported, or offered for import in any State or Territory of the United States, the District of Columbia, or the Commonwealth of Puerto Rico.

(3) In this regulation the term "where appropriate" is used several times. When a requirement is qualified by "where appropriate," it is deemed to be "appropriate" unless the manufacturer can document justification otherwise. A requirement is "appropriate" if non-implementation could reasonably be expected to result in the product not meeting its specified requirements or the manufacturer not being able to carry out any necessary corrective action.

(b) The quality system regulation in this part supplements regulations in other parts of this chapter except where explicitly stated otherwise. In the event of a conflict between applicable regulations in this part and in other parts of this chapter, the regulations specifically

applicable to the device in question shall supersede any other generally applicable requirements.

(c)Authority. Part 820 is established and issued under authority of sections 501, 502, 510, 513, 514, 515, 518, 519, 520, 522, 701, 704, 801, 803 of the act (21 U.S.C. 351, 352, 360, 360c, 360d, 360e, 360h, 360i, 360j, 360l, 371, 374, 381, 383). The failure to comply with any applicable provision in this part renders a device adulterated under section 501(h) of the act. Such a device, as well as any person responsible for the failure to comply, is subject to regulatory action.

(d)Foreign manufacturers. If a manufacturer who offers devices for import into the United States refuses to permit or allow the completion of a Food and Drug Administration (FDA) inspection of the foreign facility for the purpose of determining compliance with this part, it shall appear for purposes of section 801(a) of the act, that the methods used in, and the facilities and controls used for, the design, manufacture, packaging, labeling, storage, installation, or servicing of any devices produced at such facility that are offered for import into the United States do not conform to the requirements of section 520(f) of the act and this part and that the devices manufactured at that facility are adulterated under section 501(h) of the act.

(e)Exemptions or variances. (1) Any person who wishes to petition for an exemption or variance from any device quality system requirement is subject to the requirements of section 520(f)(2) of the act. Petitions for an exemption or variance shall be submitted according to the procedures set forth in 10.30 of this chapter, the FDA's administrative procedures. Guidance is available from the Center for Devices and Radiological Health, Division of Small Manufacturers, International and Consumer Assistance (HFZ-220), 1350 Piccard Dr., Rockville, MD 20850, U.S.A., telephone 1-800-638-2041 or 240-276-3150, FAX 240-276-3151.

(2) FDA may initiate and grant a variance from any device quality system requirement when the agency determines that such variance is in the best interest of the public health. Such variance will remain in effect only so long as there remains a public health need for the device and the device would not likely be made sufficiently available without the variance.

[61 FR 52654, Oct. 7, 1996, as amended at 65 FR 17136, Mar. 31, 2000; 65 FR 66636, Nov. 7, 2000; 69 FR 29829, May 25, 2005; 72 FR 17399, Apr. 9, 2007]

Sec. 820.3 Definitions.

(a)Act means the Federal Food, Drug, and Cosmetic Act, as amended (secs. 201-903, 52 Stat. 1040et seq., as amended (21 U.S.C. 321-394)). All definitions in section 201 of the act shall apply to the regulations in this part.

(b)Complaint means any written, electronic, or oral communication that alleges deficiencies related to the identity, quality, durability, reliability, safety, effectiveness, or performance of a device after it is released for distribution.

(c)Component means any raw material, substance, piece, part, software, firmware, labeling, or assembly which is intended to be included as part of the finished, packaged, and labeled device.

(d)Control number means any distinctive symbols, such as a distinctive combination of letters or numbers, or both, from which the history of the manufacturing, packaging, labeling, and distribution of a unit, lot, or batch of finished devices can be determined.

(e)Design history file (DHF) means a compilation of records which describes the design history of a finished device.

(f)Design input means the physical and performance requirements of a device that are used as a basis for device design.

(g)Design output means the results of a design effort at each design phase and at the end of the total design effort. The finished design output is the basis for the device master record. The total finished design output consists of the device, its packaging and labeling, and the device master record.

(h)Design review means a documented, comprehensive, systematic examination of a design to evaluate the adequacy of the design requirements, to evaluate the capability of the design to meet these requirements, and to identify problems.

(i)Device history record (DHR) means a compilation of records containing the production history of a finished device.

(j)Device master record (DMR) means a compilation of records containing the procedures and specifications for a finished device.

(k)Establish means define, document (in writing or electronically), and implement.

(l)Finished device means any device or accessory to any device that is suitable for use or capable of functioning, whether or not it is packaged, labeled, or sterilized.

(m)Lot or batch means one or more components or finished devices that consist of a single type, model, class, size, composition, or software version that are manufactured under essentially the same conditions and that are intended to have uniform characteristics and quality within specified limits.

(n)Management with executive responsibility means those senior employees of a manufacturer who have the authority to establish or make changes to the manufacturer's quality policy and quality system.

(o)Manufacturer means any person who designs, manufactures, fabricates, assembles, or processes a finished device. Manufacturer includes but is not limited to those who perform the functions of contract sterilization, installation, relabeling, remanufacturing, repacking, or specification development, and initial distributors of foreign entities performing these

functions.

(p)Manufacturing material means any material or substance used in or used to facilitate the manufacturing process, a concomitant constituent, or a byproduct constituent produced during the manufacturing process, which is present in or on the finished device as a residue or impurity not by design or intent of the manufacturer.

(q)Nonconformity means the nonfulfillment of a specified requirement.

(r)Product means components, manufacturing materials, in- process devices, finished devices, and returned devices.

(s)Quality means the totality of features and characteristics that bear on the ability of a device to satisfy fitness-for-use, including safety and performance.

(t)Quality audit means a systematic, independent examination of a manufacturer's quality system that is performed at defined intervals and at sufficient frequency to determine whether both quality system activities and the results of such activities comply with quality system procedures, that these procedures are implemented effectively, and that these procedures are suitable to achieve quality system objectives.

(u)Quality policy means the overall intentions and direction of an organization with respect to quality, as established by management with executive responsibility.

(v)Quality system means the organizational structure, responsibilities, procedures, processes, and resources for implementing quality management.

(w)Remanufacturer means any person who processes, conditions, renovates, repackages, restores, or does any other act to a finished device that significantly changes the finished device's performance or safety specifications, or intended use.

(x)Rework means action taken on a nonconforming product so that it will fulfill the specified DMR requirements before it is released for distribution.

(y)Specification means any requirement with which a product, process, service, or other activity must conform.

(z)Validation means confirmation by examination and provision of objective evidence that the particular requirements for a specific intended use can be consistently fulfilled.

(1)Process validation means establishing by objective evidence that a process consistently produces a result or product meeting its predetermined specifications.

(2)Design validation means establishing by objective evidence that device specifications conform with user needs and intended use(s).

(aa)Verification means confirmation by examination and provision of objective evidence that

10

specified requirements have been fulfilled.

Sec. 820.5 Quality system.

Each manufacturer shall establish and maintain a quality system that is appropriate for the specific medical device(s) designed or manufactured, and that meets the requirements of this part.

Takeaways from Chapter 2

There really is just one takeaway from this chapter, installing and maintaining a world-class quality management system is everything in the medical device industry. As you progress through the chapters of this book, you will find numerous warning letter extractions reflective of the FDAs stepped-up approach toward enforcement. In every single case, you will find the link back to a portion of a quality system not being implemented or even worse, not being followed. Why bother with the penning of procedures if people are not trained to procedures or expected to adhere to procedures. In some examples, you will find the complete lack of, or failure of, key elements; and in a few cases, the entire failure of a quality management system. The best advice Dr. D can offer is to invest the time in money in the quality management system up front. Why, because for organizations that don't, the FDA will make their lives miserable; and with pain comes the cost. Warning letter mitigation is expensive. You can take that to the bank as well!

Chapter 3 - Management Responsibility

21 CFR, Part 820

Subpart B

Section 820.20

Chapter 3 – Management Responsibility

Let me begin Chapter 3 by reinforcing the importance of DG Rule #1 - Compliance to regulations is not optional, compliance is mandatory and dictated by law. It is my belief; management responsibility is what the doctor likes to call the "catch-all requirement." What does that mean Dr. D? Simply put, if your organization fails to comply with any part of the QSR, rest assured, the reward will be the issuance of a Form 483 for the specific transgression, by the agency. Additionally, if the transgression can be linked back to insufficient management oversight, a second observation will be issued for ineffective management responsibility. For example, if an organization is not performing internal audits due to a lack of available resources, it is the responsibilities of management to rectify the problem by ensuring adequate resources are available. That said; please enjoy this chapter, as I dive into management responsibility.

FDA Warning Letters

Management responsibility or the lack there of, is one of the more popular Form 483 citations issued by the FDA. Additionally, the management review process is without a doubt, an area the FDA is spending some serious time reviewing during their visits. Furthermore, it is one of the key failings of the three medical device manufacturers awarded the warning letters depicted in this chapter. Remember, management reviews shall be documented, IN WRITING, and the entire management review process documented by procedure. A salient takeaway from this chapter will be, **device manufacturers do not have to share the contents of management review with the FDA!** However, they must provide sufficient proof the reviews are being held and the process is effective.

Warning Letter One (February 2010)

Failure to implement your management review procedure, as required by 21 CFR § 820.20(c). Specifically, your "Management Review" procedure, dated 8/6/07 states that management review meetings are held quarterly. Your firm has not documented a management review meeting since December 15, 2004.

Failure to establish and maintain an organizational structure to ensure that devices are designed and produced to meet the requirements of 21 CFR part 820, as required by 21 CFR § 820.20(b).

Warning Letter Two (January 2010)

Management with executive responsibility has failed to ensure that an adequate quality system, as defined in 21 CFR 820.3(v), has been fully implemented and maintained at all levels of your organization, as required by 21 CFR 820.20 as is evidenced by the observations below. In addition, your firm has not designated a management representative, as required by C.F.R. 820.20(b)(3), and you have not established management review procedures, as required by 21 C.F.R. 820.20(c), nor conducted management reviews since 2004.

Warning Letter Three (December 2009)

Failure of management with executive responsibility to review the suitability of the quality system at defined intervals and with sufficient frequency according to established procedures to ensure the quality system satisfies the requirements of this part, as required by 21 CFR 820.20(c). For example, your firm failed to establish and implement written management review procedures. The only management official on site explained he was not aware of the requirements.

Quality System Regulation 21 CFR, Part 820

QSR – Subpart B – Quality System Requirements

Section 820.20 Management Responsibility

(a)Quality policy. Management with executive responsibility shall establish its policy and objectives for, and commitment to, quality. Management with executive responsibility shall ensure that the quality policy is understood, implemented, and maintained at all levels of the organization.

(b)Organization. Each manufacturer shall establish and maintain an adequate organizational structure to ensure that devices are designed and produced in accordance with the requirements of this part.

(1)Responsibility and authority. Each manufacturer shall establish the appropriate responsibility, authority, and interrelation of all personnel who manage, perform, and assess work affecting quality, and provide the independence and authority necessary to perform these tasks.

(2)Resources. Each manufacturer shall provide adequate resources, including the assignment of trained personnel, for management, performance of work, and assessment activities, including internal quality audits, to meet the requirements of this part.

(3)Management representative. Management with executive responsibility shall appoint, and document such appointment of, a member of management who, irrespective of other responsibilities, shall have established authority over and responsibility for:
(i) Ensuring that quality system requirements are effectively established and effectively maintained in accordance with this part; and
(ii) Reporting on the performance of the quality system to management with executive responsibility for review.

(c)Management review. Management with executive responsibility shall review the suitability and effectiveness of the quality system at defined intervals and with sufficient frequency according to established procedures to ensure that the quality system satisfies the requirements of this part and the manufacturer's established quality policy and objectives. The dates and results of quality system reviews shall be documented.

(d)Quality planning. Each manufacturer shall establish a quality plan which defines the quality practices, resources, and activities relevant to devices that are designed and manufactured. The manufacturer shall establish how the requirements for quality will be met.

(e)Quality system procedures. Each manufacturer shall establish quality system procedures and instructions. An outline of the structure of the documentation used in the quality system shall be established where appropriate.

Management Responsibility

Dr. D's epistemic limits and capabilities has led him to actively pursue an unquenchable thirst in the search for meaning and understanding while dissecting the medical device industry and the regulations needed for compliance. The key components of an effective management responsibility process are; quality policy, organization structure, responsibility and authority, resources, management representative, management review, quality planning, and quality system procedures.

Let me begin with the *quality policy*. This aspect of the regulation is simple. Develop a quality policy (in writing) and ensure all employees are trained to and understand the contents of the policy. I recommend strict adherence to DG Rule # 6 – All procedures, work instructions, drawings, specifications, etc. must be written, well-documented, and controlled within a defined document control system.

The *organization* structure is also a relatively benign concept. To meet the requirement, an organization must be adequately staffed and structured to meet all of the QSR, and other FDA requirements, in support of designing and manufacturing medical devices that are safe and effective. Additionally, an organizational chart is required with evidence of an independent quality function reporting into executive management. Furthermore, the reporting structure should result in no conflicts of interest between manufacturing, quality, regulatory, and other operational functions. In short, having quality report into manufacturing is not acceptable.

Responsibility and authority are also self-evident. The quality function should have a clearly defined role that supports the organization and results in compliance with the QSR. The personnel assigned to roles within quality shall retain a sufficient level of authority and independence to address quality issues as they arise. For example, at the end of the day, you never want the manufacturing manager trumping quality-related decisions associated with non-conforming product (yes – bad example by Dr. D).

If you want to manufacture and distribute medical devices within the United States, compliance to the QSR is the price of admission. That said, it takes *resources* to comply with the regulation, and I am not just talking about quality or even quantity. Training for quality personnel performing tasks such as product assessments and internal audits is a given. It is the responsibility of management to ensure every functional area of the business is properly resourced, including janitorial services. Are you kidding me Dr. D? Seriously, it will become readily apparent, through the analysis of organizational metrics during management review, when the overall effectiveness of your organization is impaired due to resource constraints. For example, if there are cleanliness issues on the manufacturing floor (the janitor thing), the result may be an increase in contamination counts resulting in actual LAL or bio-burden issues. Remember, organizations must be properly staffed and trained.

The *management representative* is another no brainer. Select the person you want wearing the orange jumpsuit, a.k.a., the Chief Jailable Officer (CJO). Just kidding, this individual should be a senior member of the quality organization, preferably the most senior member. This individual is tasked with taking ownership of the quality system and reporting on the overall effectiveness of the quality system to management. Additionally, this position of great importance should be noted on the organizational chart. It is also expected the management representative will be an audit-facing individual, for the friendly FDA visits. Make sure this individual is trained accordingly, as the proverbial "deer in the head lights look" can result in unwanted 483s.

Management review is an often overlooked but mission critical process, as seen in the warning letters. As part of management review, all aspects of a medical device manufacturer's quality system and business system are analyzed for compliance and effectiveness. The actual review should contain sufficient granularity to ensure executive management understands the quality status of the business and can make intelligent decisions premised on the metrics provided. The key is to ensure all aspects of the quality system are reviewed for performance and ongoing compliance to the QSR. For example, and not all inclusive, critical areas requiring inclusion into the management review process should be; CAPA, supplier performance, yields, internal audits, results of external audits, training, yields, complaints, field actions, inventory issues, resources, and other significant quality and performance issues. It is up to your organization to decide what is critical and needs to be included in the review. Additionally, make sure all of the metrics being reviewed, as part of management review, are defined in the management review procedure. Furthermore, schedule and hold management reviews at published intervals. Finally, make sure there is a quorum in regards to attendance; and capture the attendance, issues, action items, etc. in the meeting minutes. Remember, the contents of management review do not have to be shared with the FDA; however, you will need to provide evidence the meetings have occurred and the process is functioning effectively.

Quality planning is a tool that defines how a medical device manufacture will meet quality requirements. The plan should contain sufficient granularity in support of defining required resources, specific activities, test methods, special testing requirements, special processes, quality practices, and similar tools needed to support the design and manufacture of medical devices. Dr. D also recommends that quality-planning documents be reviewed and approved by multiple functional organizations, placed under change control, and tracked to completion.

Lastly and probably most importantly are the *quality-system procedures*. A quality system is only as effective as the written procedures, work instructions, forms, etc. designed to support it. Dr. D strongly recommends creating a functional matrix that allows the mapping of all documentation associated with supporting your quality system back to the specific QSR requirement. The FDA references the employment of an outline of the document structure. It is Dr. D's opinion; the application of a well-designed document map will serve the same purpose. In fact, a document map with hot links is even better. Either way, the key take away for this requirement is written procedures and the organization of the document structure that depicts a cohesive approach to quality.

Takeaways from Chapter 3

Employing rocket science is not required to comply with the QSR and specifically, management responsibility. The key for complying with Section 820.20 is ensuring the management team is actively engaged in all aspects of the quality system. Consider the three warning letter excerpts presented earlier in this chapter as a forewarning from Dr. D. The effectiveness of the management review process will be evaluated by the agency, when they visit, and they will visit. A well-defined quality policy, a clear organizational structure, adequate quality resources, the identification of the management representative, defining responsibility and authority, adequate quality planning, and well-written procedures are all mission critical. Evidence of effectiveness of management responsibility, including training to the policies and procedures, shall be documented and retained. These types of records will be required to support claims of effectiveness and overall compliance to the QSR.

Remember, management responsibility is a well-defined requirement that is often overlooked by medical device manufacturers; while compliance to the QSR is mandatory. Finally, please remember, Dr. D's diatribes are being presented to enlighten and aggrandize the valued readers of this book.

Chapter 4 – Quality Audits

21 CFR, Part 820

Subpart B

Section 820.22

Chapter 4 – Quality Audits

In Chapter 4, Dr. D will provide his wisdom and insight into the requirements associated with executing effective internal quality audits. Moreover, please make no mistake, the FDA will evaluate the effectiveness of your internal quality audits and review the corrective actions pursued as part of the overall quality audit system. If a nefarious approach to executing quality audits is pursued, the reward will be a Form 483. If the FDA feels the violation is egregious, a warning letter will be forthcoming. In monopoly speak, "do not pass go and do not collect your two-hundred dollars.

FDA Warning Letters

As you can see by the abundance of warning letters issued by the agency each year, quality audits, specifically internal quality audits, are clearly on the FDA's radar screen. Once again, the failure to perform a specific task, as mandated by the Quality System Regulation (QSR), or adequate written procedures defining a specific task, has placed three organizations into the agency's doghouse. The fundamental reason behind the performance of internal quality audits is for organizations to effectively monitor and sustain ongoing compliance to the QSR; and to pursue corrective actions when non-compliances to the QSR or their internal quality procedures are observed.

Warning Letter One (February 2010)
Failure to conduct quality audits in accordance with established procedures to assure that the quality system is in compliance with the established quality system requirements and to determine the effectiveness of the quality system in accordance with 21 CFR 820.22.
- Specifically, your Internal Audit SOP requires annual internal audits; however, an internal audit has not been conducted on any quality system since October 2006.

Warning Letter Two (February 2010)
Failure to conduct an audit to assure the quality system is in compliance with the established quality system requirements, 21 CFR Part 820; and failure of your "Internal Quality Audits"

procedure, #13.1 Revision D, dated 8/06/07 to address the frequency of internal audits and assure that all parts of the quality system will be covered during the audit, as required by 21 CFR § 820.22.

Warning Letter Three (February 2010)

Failure to establish procedures for quality audits and conduct such audits to assure that the quality system is in compliance with the established quality system requirements and to determine the effectiveness of the quality system. A report of the results of each quality audit, and reaudit(s) reports shall be reviewed by management having responsibility for the matters audited as required by 21 CFR § 820.22. Specifically, your firm does not have any written procedures relating to quality audits and management reviews, and does not conduct such audits or reviews at the time of this inspection.

Quality System Regulation - 21 CFR, Part 820

QSR – Subpart B – Quality System Requirements

Section 820.22 Quality Audits

Each manufacturer shall establish procedures for quality audits and conduct such audits to assure that the quality system is in compliance with the established quality system requirements and to determine the effectiveness of the quality system. Quality audits shall be conducted by individuals who do not have direct responsibility for the matters being audited. Corrective action(s), including a reaudit of deficient matters, shall be taken when necessary. A report of the results of each quality audit, and reaudit(s) where taken, shall be made and such reports shall be reviewed by management having responsibility for the matters audited. The dates and results of quality audits and reaudits shall be documented.

Quality Audits

I am always amazed at how tasks as important as performing internal quality audits are often overlooked by medical device manufacturers or the significance and importance of audits are down played. Performing effective quality audits, and pursuing timely corrective actions, when non-compliances are noted and documented, is a sure-fire way to remain in the good graces of the agency. Additionally, performing all of the quality audits at once, i.e., within a single day or week for an entire year, is not an acceptable approach. In fact, do not buy into the shibboleth (look it up time) that performing all of the internal audits at one time, each year, equates to compliance with the QSR, Let Dr. D assure you - it does not. Furthermore, a quality audit is only a snapshot of the quality system taken at specific point in time. For example, if a quality audit on purchasing activities was performed on April 1, 2010 and there were no non-conformances noted, the conclusion drawn is that on that date, the purchasing function was in compliance with the documented quality system, procedures, and hopefully, the QSR. Finally, the individuals performing the quality audits shall be trained and shall not have direct responsibility for the area being audited. If an organization is resource challenged, the use of consultants or third-party contractors, to augment the quality audit process, is acceptable. If contractors are employed for executing internal audits, make sure these individuals are adequately trained and qualified. Make sure the credentials for consultants working as auditors are verified.

So what are the salient points associated with an effective quality audit program? It is the opinion of Dr. D, the process can be broken down into a eleven-step process (eleven is a Dr. D lucky number), with the steps of the process being:

1. The creation of a well-written procedure that delineates the quality audit process;

2. The generation and posting of the internal quality-audit schedule;

3. The training of the auditors;

4. The pre-audit meeting;

5. The actual performance of the audit;

6. The post-audit debrief;

7. The generation of the written audit report;

8. The assignment of corrective action and completion of corrective action, if warranted;

9. The verification of the effectiveness of the corrective action (follow-up audit);

10. The adjustment of the audit schedule, if deemed necessary; and

11. The inclusion of the audit results into the management review process.

One key ingredient for a successful quality audit program is blind-faith compliance with Devine Guidance Rule # 3 - Document the results of all events in writing, because if it is not documented in writing, the event did not occur. Remember, although we all tend to categorize the friendly visits by the FDA as an audit, they are not audits. The agency performs investigations and the outcome of these investigations can result in the assessment of criminal and civil penalties. This is something to keep in mind if you can be categorized as the Chief Jailable Officer (CJO). The best defense for medical device manufacturers are clear and concise policies and procedures, internal compliance to these policies and procedures, training to these policies and procedures, and documented evidence (**IN WRITING**) of compliance to policies and procedures (hint – documented policies and procedures). Remember, medical device manufacturers retain the esemplastic (look it up) power to implement effective quality tools that result in compliance with the QSR.

Takeaways from Chapter 4

An effective system governing the execution of quality audits should be the first line of defense for medical device manufacturers. Well-trained auditors, supporting an all-encompassing approach for executing effective quality audits, provides substantial value and can result in Form 483 free investigations. Some free advice from Dr. D, even though most of my advice is free - except for my football picks, focus on quality audits. I cannot stand on my proverbial soapbox and preach enough about the benefits of these audits. As a medical device manufacturer, you want to find and fix all potential non-conformances before the agency finds them. Remember if you are the CJO; picture yourself in a bright-orange jumpsuit. The vision should keep you on the straight and narrow path of compliance.

Chapter 5 – Personnel

21 CFR, Part 820

Subpart B

Section 820.25

Chapter 5 - Personnel

The FDA's requirements for personnel are delineated within Section 820.25 In fact, Section 820.25 appears to be one of the more innocuous requirements and in the opinion Dr. D, one of the most important. Can you say training, training, and more training? Regardless, compliance to the requirement is mandated by the regulation. That said, Dr. D. would probably suffer from some level of compunctious feelings if I failed to cover all aspects of the regulations as part of this current series. As always, my goal is to enlighten, entertain, and educate the readers while limiting the Doctor's pontification episodes. In reality, training is that low hanging fruit were compliance can be achieved, with the output of an effective training program having a positive influence on manufacturing operations.

FDA Warning Letters

In support of Charter 5, it was a real stretch to find an abundance of warning letters. I had to search the FDA's warning-letter database, back to July of last year (2009) to find three events. However, please do not let the absence of documented events steer you into a false sense of security. Fact – the FDA did identify violations of Section 820.25. Fact – three medical device manufactures were identified as having inadequate systems in support of the QSR. Fact – three device manufacturers were cited specifically for training related issues. Fact – the three observations could have been avoided through the implementation of a robust quality system with an emphasis on documented training.

Warning Letter One (February 2010)

Failure to establish procedures for identifying training needs and ensure that all personnel are trained to adequately perform their assigned responsibilities, and training shall be documented as required by 21 CFR § 820.25 (b). Specifically, your firm has failed to establish procedures for identifying training needs and has also failed to record personnel training so that records can be updated and gaps in training can readily be identified and filed.

We have reviewed your response and have concluded that it is inadequate because your firm has failed to establish a training procedure that would ensure personnel adequately performed their assigned responsibilities, and were provided with information about the CGMP requirements and how their particular job functions relate to the overall quality system.

Warning Letter Two (September 2009)

Failure to adequately establish procedures for identifying training needs and ensure that all personnel are trained to adequately perform their assigned responsibilities. Training shall be documented, as required by 21 CFR 820.25(b). For example, there is no documentation of employee training for your firm's numerous procedures and work instructions that are necessary for your employees to perform their assigned responsibilities.

Warning Letter Three (July 2009)

Failure to establish procedures for identifying training needs and ensure all personnel are trained to adequately perform their assigned responsibilities and failure to document the training [21 CFR. 820.25(b)]. There are no procedures for identifying training needs, and company employees who are responsible for medical device manufacturing and complaint, CAPA, and Medical Device Report (MDR) handling are not adequately trained to ensure those duties are performed correctly.

Quality System Regulation - 21 CFR, Part 820

QSR – Subpart B – Quality System Requirements

Section 820.25 Personnel

(a)General. Each manufacturer shall have sufficient personnel with the necessary education, background, training, and experience to assure that all activities required by this part are correctly performed.

(b)Training. Each manufacturer shall establish procedures for identifying training needs and ensure that all personnel are trained to adequately perform their assigned responsibilities. Training shall be documented.

(1) As part of their training, personnel shall be made aware of device defects which may occur from the improper performance of their specific jobs.

(2) Personnel who perform verification and validation activities shall be made aware of defects and errors that may be encountered as part of their job functions.

Personnel

From Dr. D's perspective, the guidance provided for this chapter falls into the category of the proverbial "no-brainer." Why – because the QSR is crystal-clear as it delineates the requirements; (a) a sufficient number of personnel; (b) that possess the education, experience, background, and training to ensure work is performed correctly; (c) training procedures are established; and the training is documented.

Additionally, when device defects, non-conformances, and associated anomalies are the result of the improper execution of a specific job task, the individuals performing these tasks, shall be made aware of their errors. Years ago, as a young US Marine, Dr. D. would use a 30-day assignment to the chow hall (scrubbing pots and pans) to reinforce training issues; however, not practical in today's medical device industry. That said, documented retraining with a follow-up evaluation and a supervisor's additional oversight of the offending individual's work should suffice.

Furthermore, the same basic requirement is applicable to individuals tasked with executing verification and validation protocols. These individuals must also remain informed in regards to defects and errors.

Finally, one tool that Dr. D. found particularly effective was public floggings in the back parking lot (just kidding). It was in the front parking lot. Seriously, I found a weekly review of complaint data, mixed with some good-natured needling of the offending / responsible R & D, quality, and manufacturing engineers, on a Friday afternoon, to be a nice proactive approach for identifying real product issues. The information gleaned from these brainstorming sessions can be shared with the operators, technicians, and inspectors. The result is a cohesive teaming approach to manufacturing medical devices that are safe and effective. Additionally, Dr. D is a believer of a simple rule (probably would qualify for DG. rule); all managers and above, regardless of responsibility, should walk the manufacturing floor at least once each week. If you are a manager tasked with overseeing production, quality, engineering, etc. the walk really needs to be daily. Furthermore, trust your employees and staff. My 30-plus years of experience (yes Dr. D is old) tells me that if an assembler or inspector identifies ways to improve a process, listen to them as they live and breathe manufacturing day in and day out.

Takeaways from Chapter 5

In wrapping up Chapter 5, the key takeaway needs to be the training piece. Ensuring adequate training cascades through all levels of the organization is of significant importance. Documented evidence of training to ensure employees, contractors, consultants, etc. can adequately execute assigned tasks associated with medical device manufacturing is a prerequisite. The expectation is that all individuals associated with device manufacturing understand the QSR, as it influences their particular job function. Remember, the agency can and will issue Form 483s for all noted violations.

Chapter 6 – Design Controls

21 CFR, Part 820

Subpart C

Section 820.30

Chapter 6 – Design Controls

The design control requirements delineated within 21 CFR, Part 820 - Section 820.30 continue to drive a significant level of consternation for the medical device industry. The regulation is very specific in regards to the elements required for an effective design control process. Long gone are the days of working off the proverbial napkin drawings or the concept of a freewheeling research and development (R & D) group operating in the proverbial vacuum. In today's medical device manufacturing environment, the FDA expects compliance with all aspects of 21 CFR, Part 820. Yes – I know Dr. D is probably sounding like a broken record; however, failure to adhere with DG Rule # 1 – Compliance to regulations is not optional, compliance is mandatory and dictated by law; and you will find your organization facing the wrath of the agency.

FDA Warning Letters

While surfing the FDA's warning letter database, the violations noted against design control and documented within FDA issued warning letters were numerous. In fact, the FDA is so concerned about design control and the overall effect design control exudes on the safety and efficacy of medical devices, it is possible to receive several Form 483 observations for failing to comply with multiple subsections of design control.

FDA Warning Letter One

The offending manufacturer, depicted in warning letter violation one, received a warning letter containing six (6) specific violations of the code, including subsections. Premised on this warning letter extraction, the investigator was thoroughly displeased with the level of compliance exhibited by this medical device manufacturer.

Warning Letter (March 2010)

1. Failure to establish and maintain adequate procedures to ensure that the design requirements relating to a device are appropriate and address the intended use of the device, including the needs of the user and patient, as required by 21 CFR 820.30(c). For example procedures for Version (b)(4) EGG machine in (b)(4) or for the upgrade made to the Research Version device in (b)(4) which included a new Research Waterload Version and a Waterload Version.

2. Failure to establish and maintain adequate procedures for defining and documenting design output in terms that allow an adequate evaluation of conformance to design input requirements, as required by 21 CFR 820.30(d). For example:

> *a. When requested, design output procedures and/or requirements for the upgrade from Version (b)(4) to Version (b)(4) done by (b)(4) and for the upgrade from Version (b)(4) Research device to Versions (b)(4) Research, Research Waterload device done (b)(4) could not be provided.*
> *b. When requested, no evidence that design outputs were established and evaluated against design inputs document (b) (4) was provided.*
> *c. There is no record of review and approval of device labeling, including review and approval of the labeling for the Research Version (b) (4) released (b) (4)*

3. Failure to establish and maintain adequate procedures to ensure that formal documented reviews of the design results are planned and conducted at appropriate stages of the device's design development, as required by 21 CFR 820.30(e). For example, procedures were not established to ensure formal documented reviews of the design during the design planning process.

4. Failure to establish and maintain adequate procedures for verifying the device design and documenting the results of the design verification, including identification of the design, method(s), the date, and the individual(s) performing the verification, as required by 21 CFR820.30(t). For example:

> *a. When requested, no documentation to confirm that the finished product conformed to specified requirement as stated in the (b) (4) was provided.*
> *b. The design plan identifies what testing will be done to ensure general assembly requirements are met; however, when requested, the documentation to support testing that was performed on the following activities could not be located: (1) 'Test Type CF EGG Lead on CWE Head Stage," (2) "Test Type B on Respiration Connection" and (3) "Verify Cart - Tip Test."*

5. Failure to establish and maintain adequate procedures for validating the device design, as required by 21 CFR 820.30(g). For example:

> *a. When requested no evidence to show that the validation test was performed as stated in Test Report (b) (4) was provided.*
> *b. When requested, no evidence to support that the finished device was validated to include validation with the EGGSAS software was provided.*
> *c. The Failure Modes Effect Analysis FMEA described in (b) (4) does not define the Average Likelihood of Occurrence (ALOO) for each value.*

6. Failure to establish and maintain procedures for the identification, documentation, validation or where appropriate verification, review, and approval of design changes before their implementation, as required by 21 CFR 820.30(i). For example:

> *a. When requested, no procedure identifying how design changes made to the device are processed was provided.*
> *b. When requested, no evidence that the changes made to the finished device or the research, research waterload, or waterload software versions were verified or validated to ensure that the changes are effective and did not adversely affect the finished product was provided.*
> *c. When requested, no evidence to support the device software update from Research Version (b)(4) to Version (b)(4) was verified to meet design requirements as stated in the (b)(4) was provided.*
> *d. When requested, no documentation to support that the changes to EGGSAS software were verified to demonstrate the functionality was provided. The EGGSAS version (b)(4) software is the software component for the EGG machine that is used in conjunction with the (b) (4) to provide a diagnosis of gastric motility disorders.*

FDA Warning Letter Two

Since I began penning this book in late 2010, I have continued to pontificate in regards to the importance of having written policies and procedures. In just about ever- single warning letter I have ever read, a common thread, observed in warning letters, is the lack of procedures or compliance with procedures. I guess I have some difficulty in comprehending how a medical device manufacturer can fail to grasp a simple concept such as having **WRITTEN PROCEDURES! HELLO!** Now that Dr. D has gotten that out of his system. In this warning letter extraction, multiple violations are noted against the FDA's design control requirements, including the lack of **WRITTEN PROCEDURES! HELLO!**

Warning Letter (February 2010)

> *Failure to establish and maintain procedures to control the design of the device in order to ensure that specified design requirements are met as required by 21 CFR § 820.30(a). Specifically, your firm has no design control procedures to control the design process of your device. Your firm has failed to establish a plan for the changes made to your MICRON 400 UV & 800 UV devices to determine the adequacy of the design requirements and to ensure that the design that was released to production meets the approved requirements.*

Failure to establish and maintain procedures for the identification, documentation, validation or where appropriate verification, review, and approval of design changes before their implementation as required by 21 CFR § 820.30(i). Specifically, your firm has failed to establish and maintain design control procedures for the design changes that were made to your devices during the months of May and June of 2009. For example, your firm has made changes to the design of your MICRON 400 UV & 800UV devices by adding an (b)(4) in order to verify that the UV lamps inside the device were in working condition, and also a (b)(4) to turn off or not turn on the (b)(4) when the HEPA filter is being replaced. Your firm must establish a criterion for evaluating changes in order to ensure that the changes are appropriate for its designs.

Failure to establish and maintain a design history file (DHF) for each type of device as required by 21 CFR § 820.30(j). Specifically, there were no design history files for the following devices: MICROCON 400M, 400UV, 800M, 800UV, WallMAP, WallMAP PC, Ex-BB, and ExC-BB. For example, your MICROCON 800M PREPARATION LIST does not contain or reference the records necessary to demonstrate that the design was developed in accordance with the approved design plan and the requirements of this part (21 CFR § 820.30). Your firm has failed to document the complete history of the design process where such records are necessary to ensure that the final design will conform to the design specifications.

FDA - Response: *We have reviewed your response and have concluded that it is inadequate because there is no indication that you have implemented adequate written procedures to address the design control violations documented by our FDA Investigator on the FDA-483 that was issued to you.*

FDA Warning Letter Three

Finding warning letters for violations of 21 CFR, Part 820, section 820.3 is child's play, due the bountiful amount of warning-letter observations. The FDA's warning-letter database is loaded with violators of the design and development requirement. In this warning letter extraction, the offending medical device manufacturer has attempted to meet some of the design and development requirements; however, there are disconnects between the requirements and the supporting data. Additionally, verification of the requirements is missing. Another point Dr. D is compelled to make is evidence of compliance. Later in this book, Dr. D. will present the ins and outs of responding to Form 483s and warning letters. However, one very basic key is the providing of objective evidence. In God we trust, all others bring data; the FDA's policy is quite similar.

Warning Letter (February 2010)

1. Failure to establish and maintain adequate procedures to ensure that the design requirements relating to a device are appropriate and address the intended use of the device, and include a mechanism for addressing incomplete, ambiguous, or conflicting requirements, as required by 21 CFR 820.30(c). For example:

a. Section 16.3.2 of the document 102-0083 Rev A, Product Requirements Document PH AED 2 (G3), states that the battery shall be designed to have adequate capacity for a guaranteed three year operating life under normal use conditions. However, the document does not define what constitutes the "operating life under normal conditions."

We have reviewed your response and have concluded that the adequacy of your response cannot be determined at this time. You indicated that by November 13, 2009, you would update the design input requirements to eliminate conflicting and/or ambiguous language and the battery will be reverified against the revised input documents. You have not, however, provided any evidence of implementation of this corrective action.

*b. Section 5.3 of the document DHF-00048-01, G3 AED **(b) (4)** Battery Product Design Inputs, lists the physical specifications of the battery. According to the specification, operating ambient temperature is specified as 0°C to 50°C. However, the electrical specifications, listed in section 5.4 of the document, lists the operating temperature as 25°C.*

We have reviewed your response and have concluded that the adequacy of your response cannot be determined at this time. You indicated that by November 13, 2009, you would update the design input requirements to eliminate conflicting and/or ambiguous language and the battery will be reverified against the revised input documents. You have not, however, provided any evidence of implementation of this corrective action.

2. Failure to establish and maintain adequate procedures to confirm that design output meets the design input requirements, as required by 21 CFR 820.30(f). For example, section 16.3.1 of the document 102-0083 Rev A, Product Requirements Document PH AED 2 (G3), states that the battery shall be designed to have adequate capacity for 300 shocks (typical). However, no documented verification was performed to ensure such capacity.

We have reviewed your response and have concluded that the adequacy of your response cannot be determined at this time. You indicated that by November 13, 2009, you would update the design input requirements to eliminate conflicting and/or ambiguous language and that as a result you will also reverify the battery against the revised input documents. You have not, however, provided any evidence of implementation of this corrective action.

FDA Warning Letter Four

In this example of an FDA warning letter extraction, the offending medical device manufacturer received five (5) observations against their design control process. The

FDA cited issues with validations (subsection g), design changes (subsection i), design

output (sub-section d), design review (subsection e), and maintaining the DHF

(subsection j). Overall, the FDA was extremely displeased with this organization's

commitment to design control and compliance with the QSR; and rewarded the

organization accordingly, for their general lack of compliance.

Warning Letter (December 2009)

1. Failure to adequately establish and maintain procedures for validating the device design, as required by 21 CFR 820.30(g). For example:

> *a. Protocol (b)(4), Stability Testing - Drugs of Abuse Products," issued 11/20/2000 states that during a (b)(4) Stress Stability Study testing should continue at (b)(4) However, Form (b)(4)"Stability Study Testing Schedule," dated 02/07/2003 shows that the (b)(4) testing for the Fastect II device (cat # (b)(4) was only performed at start, week (b)(4) and week (b)(4). The study was finished and approved at week (b) (4) without observing (b) (4).*

> *B. Protocol (b) (4) "Stability Testing - Drugs of Abuse Products," issued 11/20/2000 states that (b) (4) lots of a device must pass (b) (4) and (b)(4) storage stability studies to validate and/or change the shelf life claim. The oven stress testing (b) (4) should continue (b) (4). However, Form (b)(4), rev C, "Stability Study Testing Schedule," completed on 08/18/2003 shows that the (b)(4) testing for the Fastect II device (cat#(b)(4))was performed using only one lot and only performed at start, weeks (b)(4) and (b)(4). The study was finished and approved at week (b) (4) without observing (b) (4).*

> *c. When requested, no accelerated or real time stability studies were provided to support the QuickTox Multi Drug Dipcard's expiration date.*

> *d. Protocol (b)(4), rev. C, "Stability Testing - Urine Drugs of Abuse Products," issued 01/16/2004 states that during a (b)(4) Temperature Stability Study testing should continue at monthly intervals until the (b)(4) for (b)(4) consecutive months or until product (b)(4) months storage. The procedure only requires that the test be read at (b) (4) minutes. However, the device's instructions for use indicate that the test can be read up to 60 minutes.*

> *e. Document (b)(4), Rev. A, "MET-500 Shelf-Life Stability Study," dated 4/01/2000 and Document (b)(4),Rev. A, "MTD: Shelf-Life Stability Study," dated 4/01/2000 indicate that the product should be tested at monthly intervals (b)(4) However, test results show that the studies were stopped at (b)(4) and (b)(4) weeks respectively (b)(4).*

f. The firm's Fastect II, Fastect II CLIA Waived, and QuickTox device package inserts include claims for accuracy and precision, and read-time. When requested, no raw data, protocols, or final reports were provided to support these claims.

g. The real time stability study to extend the shelf-life of the Fastect II device from (b) (4) months to (b) (4) months is dated 5/9/2008. However, the raw data is dated 6/24/2008 and 2/12/2009.

2. Failure to adequately establish and maintain procedures for the identification, documentation, validation or where appropriate verification, review, and approval of design changes before their implementation, as required by 21 CFR 820.30(i). For example:

a. The firm submitted a Special 510(k) submission on July 15, 2009, to (b) (4) the Monitect Single Drug Screen Dipstick Test into the QuickTox Multiple Drug Dipcard and to (b) (4) the test strips.

When requested, the firm did not provide any verification or validation protocols or data to support these changes.

b. The firm notified FDA on February 25, 2005, of a modification to the QuickTox Multi Drug Dipcard. The new device, the Fastect II Drug Screen Dipstick Test, was a change from a dipcard to a (b) (4). When requested, the firm did not provide any verification or validation protocols or data to support this change.

c. "Project 004 (Fastect II - CLIA. Waive)" includes a change in the (b) (4) of the Fastect II strips and holder from (b) (4) to (b) (4). When requested, the firm did not provide any verification or validation protocols or data to support this change.

d. The firm notified FDA on October 16, 2002, of (b) (4) to the QuickTox Multi Drug Dipcard. Changes to the device included (b) (4) for (b) (4) and (b) (4) from (b) (4) to (b) (4) and (b) (4) to (b) (4) respectively. When requested, the firm did not provide any verification or validation protocols or data to support this change.

3. Failure to adequately establish and maintain procedures for defining and documented design output including documenting, reviewing, and approving design outputs before release, as required by 21 CFR 820.30(d). For example, Form (b) (4), Rev. A, "Product Technical Specifications (PTS)," dated 4/09/2004 for the CLIA Waive Fastect II device does not document any design outputs. When questioned, the firm stated that they did not establish any final design outputs.

4. Failure to adequately establish and maintain procedures to ensure that formal documented reviews for the design results are planned and conducted at appropriate stages of the device's design development, as required by 21 CFR 820.30(e). For example, the design history file for "Project 004 (Fastect II - CLIA Waive)" does not contain documented design reviews for Phase IV Pre-Production, Phase V Design Verification, or Phase VI Design Validation.

5. Failure to establish and maintain a design history file for each type of device, as required by 21 CFR 820.30(j). For example, when requested, the firm indicated that they did not establish a design history file for the QuickTox Multi Drug Dipcard.

Quality System Regulation - 21 CFR, Part 820

QSR – Subpart C – Design Controls

Section 820.30 Design Controls

(a)General. *(1) Each manufacturer of any class III or class II device, and the class I devices listed in paragraph (a)(2) of this section, shall establish and maintain procedures to control the design of the device in order to ensure that specified design requirements are met. (2) The following class I devices are subject to design controls:*
(i) Devices automated with computer software; and
(ii) The devices listed in the following chart.

Section	*Device*
868.6810	*Catheter, Tracheobronchial Suction.*
878.4460	*Glove, Surgeon's.*
880.6760	*Restraint, Protective.*
892.5650	*System, Applicator, Radionuclide, Manual.*
892.5740	*Source, Radionuclide Teletherapy.*

(b)Design and development planning. *Each manufacturer shall establish and maintain plans that describe or reference the design and development activities and define responsibility for implementation. The plans shall identify and describe the interfaces with different groups or activities that provide, or result in, input to the design and development process. The plans shall be reviewed, updated, and approved as design and development evolves.*

(c)Design input. *Each manufacturer shall establish and maintain procedures to ensure that the design requirements relating to a device are appropriate and address the intended use of the device, including the needs of the user and patient. The procedures shall include a mechanism for addressing incomplete, ambiguous, or conflicting requirements. The design input requirements shall be documented and shall be reviewed and approved by a designated individual(s). The approval, including the date and signature of the individual(s) approving the requirements, shall be documented.*

(d)Design output. *Each manufacturer shall establish and maintain procedures for defining and documenting design output in terms that allow an adequate evaluation of conformance to design input requirements. Design output procedures shall contain or*

make reference to acceptance criteria and shall ensure that those design outputs that are essential for the proper functioning of the device are identified. Design output shall be documented, reviewed, and approved before release. The approval, including the date and signature of the individual(s) approving the output, shall be documented.

(e)Design review. Each manufacturer shall establish and maintain procedures to ensure that formal documented reviews of the design results are planned and conducted at appropriate stages of the device's design development. The procedures shall ensure that participants at each design review include representatives of all functions concerned with the design stage being reviewed and an individual(s) who does not have direct responsibility for the design stage being reviewed, as well as any specialists needed. The results of a design review, including identification of the design, the date, and the individual(s) performing the review, shall be documented in the design history file (the DHF).

(f)Design verification. Each manufacturer shall establish and maintain procedures for verifying the device design. Design verification shall confirm that the design output meets the design input requirements. The results of the design verification, including identification of the design, method(s), the date, and the individual(s) performing the verification, shall be documented in the DHF.

(g)Design validation. Each manufacturer shall establish and maintain procedures for validating the device design. Design validation shall be performed under defined operating conditions on initial production units, lots, or batches, or their equivalents. Design validation shall ensure that devices conform to defined user needs and intended uses and shall include testing of production units under actual or simulated use conditions. Design validation shall include software validation and risk analysis, where appropriate. The results of the design validation, including identification of the design, method(s), the date, and the individual(s) performing the validation, shall be documented in the DHF.

(h)Design transfer. Each manufacturer shall establish and maintain procedures to ensure that the device design is correctly translated into production specifications.

(i)Design changes. Each manufacturer shall establish and maintain procedures for the identification, documentation, validation or where appropriate verification, review, and approval of design changes before their implementation.

(j)Design history file. Each manufacturer shall establish and maintain a DHF for each type of device. The DHF shall contain or reference the records necessary to demonstrate that the design was developed in accordance with the approved design plan and the requirements of this part.

Design Control

Design controls are far too important a topic for Dr. D. to breakdown and provide

wisdom in just a few brief paragraphs. I would never want R & D engineers to heap contumely on the good doctor for potentially presenting concepts and opinions obverse to their own beliefs. That said, the doctor has invested a significant amount of time and prose to ensure design control is adequately covered in Chapter 6.

General (a)

The regulation specifically requires that medical device manufacturers to establish, in writing I might add (broken record time again), procedures that delineate the manufacturer's specific requirements for designing Class II and Class III medical devices, and Class I devices, as depicted in the table under the regulation section of this chapter. Basically, the agency wants to ensure all of the design requirements, for medical devices, are achieved. The fundamental logic imposed here is quite simple, Dr. D. believes, "adherence to a strong design control philosophy will result in the development of medical devices that are safe and effective." Additionally, most medical device manufacturers employ the concept of a market specification, and not a napkin drawing to convey the basic requirements for a device. Furthermore, the market specification drives the specific product and design requirements that ultimately reside within the product specification. Finally, the product specification drives the design verification and validation testing and delineates all of the critical characteristics that require monitoring throughout the entire design, development, manufacturing, and post-market surveillance processes.

All of the specifications, drawings, test results, reports, validations, inspections etc., in support of design, need a home. In the eyes of the FDA, this home is the Design History File, a.k.a. – the DHF. Rest assured, the agency will review DHFs during each friendly visit; and may make the review of the DHF the omphalos (look it up if you have to) of their visit. Remember, the DHF is a dynamic receptacle for documents. The FDA requires all relevant information influencing the device design to be captured during the entire product life cycle, including product labeling, with the resultant data, reports, etc. placed into the DHF and **retained** as proof of compliance. Just like any process a good rule of thumb to remember is, "garbage in equates to garbage out."

Design and Development Planning (b)

The path toward compliance with subpart b is the creation of a fundamentally sound plan for design and development. The design and development plan should contain sufficient granularity in regards to clearly specifying all of the required deliverables associated with a specific design project. Additionally, the design and development plan is a controlled document and should be reviewed and approved by a cross-functional team. For example, R & D, quality, manufacturing, regulatory affairs, clinical, marketing, etc., should have input and ultimate approval authority for this plan. Furthermore, management should also be included in the approval cycle. Management inclusion ensures there will be no surprises when the design reviews are held. Finally, ensure the plan becomes a part of the DHF.

So what are the salient deliverables associated with a well-defined design and development plan? From Dr. D's perspective, first and foremost, a project charter and contract are warranted. These documents delineated scope of the program, deliverables, timelines, exemptions, etc. The doctor strongly recommends that all project team members, stakeholders, and the appropriate management representatives review and approve the contract. The next phase is to create an actual design and development plan. Dr. D has witnessed multiple approaches to the design and development of medical

42

devices. Some organizations create a high-level project plan that points to subservient plans for accomplishing specific tasks, e.g., design validation, quality, regulatory, etc. I prefer one plan that contains sufficient granularity to support the design and development process, while complying with QSR requirements. Besides, all of the protocols and reports will be individual deliverables anyway. As part of the design and development plan, the following list captures potential activities that should be assessed (not an all-inclusive list) for inclusion into the plan:

1. Design verification activities;

2. Design validation activities;

3. Quality requirements;

4. Regulatory requirements;

5. Creation of the Design History File;

6. Design approval and transfer activities;

7. Labeling requirements;

8. Clinical requirements;

9. Special testing requirements, e.g., DEHP; and

10. All additional requirements deemed relevant by the project team.

Remember, adhering to a robust design and development process should result in the design of a quality medical device that is safe and effective.

Design Input (c)

A fundamental concept associated with the design input requirement is the need to understand that design input equates to design requirements. As mentioned previously, the market specification and the product specification are two key design input deliverables. Medical device manufacturers need to ensure that the device requirements defined as part of the overall design and development process are appropriate for the device. As a minimum, the requirements must focus on the intended use of the device, the user requirements for the device, and the person on the receiving end of the treatment, a.k.a., the patient. For example, if your organization is developing catheters for the treatment of arrhythmias, some of the design inputs evaluated for consideration might be rigidity of the catheter shaft, insertion force into the introducer sheath, maneuverability of the catheter in the right atrium, or the potential length of the procedure. A test for analyzing the impact of leaving the catheter in the body for 30-days is probably not a realistic input requirement. Additionally, design inputs must be captured in a written document. That document needs to be reviewed and approved by the appropriate level of authority within the organization, including all of the usual suspects, R & D, quality, regulatory, marketing, medical sciences, manufacturing, etc.; and make sure each approval signature is accompanied by a date.

Furthermore, procedures associated with design control; and specifically design inputs need to have a feedback loop built into the document. The feedback-loop can be employed as a vehicle for addressing incomplete, ambiguous, or conflicting requirements. Dr. D. loves flow charts; and creating one as part of the design control process is strongly recommended.

Finally, guess where all of the documents and deliverables associated with defining the design inputs are going to be stored? Can you say Design History File (DHF)? Dr. D knew you could. All kidding aside, as you continue through the entire design control and development process, the DHF becomes a living receptacle, capturing the entire process. Remember, the FDA will dive into the DHF, either at submission time or during one of their friendly visits; so it should be deemed a mission-critical activity keeping the contents of the DHF current...

Design Output (d)

The logical predecessor to the design input is a design output; and yes, Dr. D thought that up all by himself. Claiming the "this is not rocket science clause" the design outputs consists of determining if the design inputs meet their predefined requirements. Sounds pretty simple, right? Dr. D would like to introduce a new FDA acronym now. The Device Master Record (DMR) can be categorized as a design output document, along with all of the protocols and validations that will be employed to verify the design inputs. As part of the evaluation of design inputs and the resultant outputs, the acceptance criteria employed as part of evaluating the design outputs must be defined. For example, using the catheter example, working length is probably important. Defining how the working length will be evaluated becomes part of the design output. If the catheter's working length is 100cm long, employing a 6-inch steel rule for ascertaining the actual working length is probably not a reasonable approach. In fact, have fun validating that test method. Once the quality manager stops laughing hysterically, he or she will probably throw you out of their office. Similar to the previous section on design input, all characteristics that reflect the proper operation of the proposed design need to be identified and validated. Additionally, the design outputs shall be documented, and the results reviewed, approved, signed, dated, etc. Similar to the design input deliverables, all design output documentation and deliverables shall be placed securely into the DHF. Can you see the trend?

Design Review (e)

Medical devices are typically not designed or developed in a short period of time or in a vacuum. The design and development process typically occurs in phases with actual stop gates put into place so reviews can be held to ascertain the progress against the actual design and development plan. Design reviews are employed as tools to ensure adequate oversight is exuded over the entire design process, from design inception to initial market release. As a medical device manufacturer, you never want to reach a point in the design and development process where: (a) the organization finally realizes that too much money has been spent; (b) the device will never work as designed; or even worse, (c) there is no potential to make any possible return on the investment, regardless of the benefits of the newly designed medical device.

That said, design reviews need to be a structured event with all of the key stakeholders in attendance. Attendance should be mandatory and if a quorum is not in attendance, the review needs to be rescheduled; and remember to send out flame mails to the offending individuals that failed to make attending the review a priority. Dr. D strongly recommends allowing outsiders, no not competitors, or family members, but organizational members not connected to the specific design and development project to attend the reviews. For example, a manufacturing supervisor, inspection supervisor, clinical affairs person, procurement manager, or an individual not close to the project may bring some additional insight into the review that the design team may have missed. You may need to add a specialist such as a polymer engineer, chemist, toxicologist, etc. to support the review. Now comes Dr. D's broken record time. The entire design review process shall be documented by a **WRITTEN PROCEDURE;** and the entire design review captured in meeting minutes, including the results of the review, decisions made, attendees, dates, etc. and placed into the DHF.

Design Verification (f)

Design verification activities measure and confirm that design-output requirements meet the design-input requirements that are depicted within the product specification. Test protocols, test reports, procedures, test methods, and all documentation associated with ensuring that design inputs and outputs that support the validity of the product specification are executed and collected as part of design validation. Similar to all of the deliverables delineated within the design and development requirements of the regulation, the DHF becomes the appropriate receptacle for storage. Additionally, all of the documentation, evidence, reports, etc. must be reviewed and approved by the appropriate level of authority, while making sure signatures and dates are included.

Design Validation (g)

Broken record time again - design validation, like all of the requirements within the regulation; require procedures for validating all of the features of the device design. One additional and extremely important requirement is the conditions under which design validations should be executed. For starters, design validation testing needs to occur on units manufactured under normal manufacturing conditions, preferably, (as the FDA words it) on the initial production units, lots, or batches. The salient objective of the entire design validation process is to ensure medical devices conform to their intended use. This includes all user needs and intended uses, as defined in the approved market specification.

Once all design validation activities have been completed, can you guess where all of the approved, signed, and dated documentation is stored? Yes, the DHF is the million-dollar response – good. Just like all of the deliverables required under design and development, granularity in the protocols and accurate reports are important pieces of evidence. Dr. D strongly recommends the creation and employment of test data sheets to collect test results obtained while executing protocols. Some important elements recommended for inclusion into the data sheets and needed for the reports are:

1. Protocol number;

2. List of test equipment employed, including calibration status;

3. Sample sizes and sample-size rationale;

4. Name of technician or engineer executing a specific test;

5. Signature and date of technician or engineer;

6. Date the test was executed;

7. Noted test anomalies;

8. Clearly defined pass or fail statements;

9. Limits;

10. Part Number being tested, including batch; and

11. Other test information deemed relevant by the protocol.

Design Transfer (h)

So when does the actual transfer of a newly designed medical device occur? According to Dr. D, design transfer occurs after the successful completion of all verification and validation activities. Typically, the decision to transfer is made during the final design review. As part of this last design review, the team will make the decision to transfer the design to manufacturing and the eventual commercialization. Another important milestone needing to occur, prior to the design transfer, is the completion of all documentation needed in support of the successful manufacture of the newly designed medical device. For example, all assembly drawings, bills of material, routers, special processes, inspection criteria, test criteria, acceptance criteria, etc. must be approved and released within the document control system. Additionally, Dr. D. insists that all procured material that will be employed in the manufacture of the newly designed medical device must successfully pass First Article Inspection (FAI) and subsequent receiving inspection. That said, the documentation required as part of the design transfer should encompass the purchasing and receiving inspection processes specific to the newly designed device. Finally, please ensure your regulatory affairs group has received proper clearance, PMA, 510(k), or IDE, prior to moving into commercialization; otherwise, you will need to commit to memory a very bad six-letter word **RECALL**!

Design Changes (i)

I find it amazing that medical device manufacturers continue to make changes to their devices, while failing to properly validate changes, or worst yet, failing to notify the agency when significant changes are made. As many of you are already aware, Boston Scientific Corporation voluntarily withdrew their implantable devices in March of 2010, when design (process) changes were made, and the changes not reported to the agency, via a PMA supplement, for the agency's review and approval. The PMA supplement was quickly assembled and submitted to the agency. The agency completed their review within 30-days and issued their formal approval. Dr. D's rule of thumb is to become friendly with the local office of the FDA and ask for guidance when the magnitude of a proposed design or process change is in question. If the FDA recommends filing a 30-day supplement for a PMA device, you file. There is no need for further discussion. Broken record time again - this is not rocket science, as the requirements for design control are cut and dry. That said, regardless of device classification or regulatory path for clearance, all design changes need to be assessed for impact to the finished medical device, including; (a) the impact to the device user, (b) the impact to the overall safety and efficacy of the device, and (c) the regulatory impact in regards to review and approval of all changes by the agency. Regulatory assessments should be performed by regulatory affairs' specialists, novel concept right? Dr. D recommends creating a form for completing regulatory assessments. Additionally, ensure regulatory affairs' specialists are reviewers and signatories on all design changes, period! Furthermore, regulatory assessments should become an attachment is support of all documentation associated with each design change. Finally, broken record time - when in doubt - contact your local FDA office, when there is a question or concern pertaining to the specific regulatory path, in regards to notifying the FDA over potential design changes.

Design History File (j)

Lastly but surely not the least important requirement associated with design control is the DHF, which I have previously mentioned while dissecting design control. The DHF is the receptacle for all documentation associated with the entire design and development process, including design changes made after design transfer. Documentation placed into the DHF should include (not an all-inclusive list):

1. Design & Development Plan;

2. Market Specification;

3. Product Specification;

4. Verification Protocols;

5. Validation Protocols;

6. All Procedures Defining the Design & Development Process;

7. Design Reviews;

8. Test Reports;

9. Drawings;

10. Specifications;

11. Bill of Materials;

12. Routers;

13. Subsequent Design and Process Changes; and

14. All remaining Documentation related Device Design and Development.

Takeaways from Chapter 6

There is no perfect model in regards to the design and development process, only a compliant model. Contents of the design control system will be driven in part due to organizational structure and the type of medical device being designed. The key for compliance to the regulation and the successful design and development of a medical device, that is safe and effective, is the planning. As always, detailed and accurate documentation is required to support claims of compliance to the QSR. The agency will want to review the DHF, especially if product problems result in recalls. Remember, DG Rule # 3 - Document the results of all events in writing, because if it is not documented, in writing, the event did not occur.

Additionally, I do not find compliance to the quality system regulations particularly challenging or complex. Compliance, Dr. D's opinion, is premised on well-written procedures, training, accurate documentation/records, and the ability to pursue corrective action when systemic adjustments are warranted. Effective design control essentially contains these same four elements. An effective design and development process results in the creation of medical devices that are safe and effective.

Furthermore, the primary deliverable and output, for design verification and design validation activities, is the verification that design output requirements meet design input requirements. The overall verification and validation of the information depicted within the product specification and market specification is extremely important. At this point of the design and development process, an organization needs to ensure the newly designed medical devices meet all of their predetermined requirements, including user and intended use needs. As with all of the requirements, documentation and retention are important actions that are needed to support proof of compliance, aka evidence. The DHF, when employed properly, will become an invaluable tool in supporting claims of compliance.

Finally, work associated with the design and development of medical devices does not end with the transfer of the design to manufacturing and the subsequent introduction of the device into commerce. In fact, design changes and updates to the DHF will continue throughout the entire life of the medical device. In reality, the design and development process becomes a womb to tomb scenario. Significant attention to detail should be given to actual design transfer activities. There are few things more frustrating for the production department then the receipt of a newly designed device that cannot be manufactured in accordance with the recently released transfer package, due to errors or omissions within the bills of material, routers, assembly instructions, etc. Remember, when design and/or process changes are warranted, ensure the regulatory affair's group performs an adequate assessment of the changes and adheres to the proper path for FDA notification. Equally important - the DHF. The DHF needs to be sustained until the last medical device is entered into commerce and/or consumed, and then some. In short, Dr. D calls the DHF a forever document; and the primary source of evidence for proving compliance to the design control requirements of the regulation.

Chapter 7 – Document Controls

21 CFR, Part 820

Subpart D

Section 820.40

Chapter 7 – Document Controls

The control of documentation is one the fundamental cornerstones supporting the foundation needed for an effective quality system, whether compliance is to EN ISO 13485, EN ISO 9000, the Medical Device Directive, or in the case of this book, the Quality System Regulation (QSR). Additionally, the system employed for document controls must be all-encompassing in regards to capability, e.g., document creation, storage, issuance, changes, reviews, approvals, etc. Furthermore, the system employed for document controls must be able to handle all types of documentation, i.e., procedures, forms, reports, drawings, specifications, etc. Moreover, the system needs to efficiently and effectively process change requests, including signatures and dates of approvers. Finally, all aspects of the system employed for document controls must be fully documented, by **WRITTEN PROCEDURE,** with the ability to ensure only approved documents are released for use. One final point, record retention, e.g., all documents, must be maintained. The FDA will assess the effectiveness of document controls as part of their friendly visit; and verify the adequacy of your system, premised on a review of the records being maintained. Remember, records are evidence and support compliance or potentially, the lack of compliance.

FDA Warning Letter

As I stated in the introduction to this chapter, document control is really the cornerstone and foundation for an effective quality system. In fact, the regulation depicts two salient points; (a) approval signatures are required, and (b) dates of approval are required. In this chapter's FDA warning letter extraction, the offending medical device manufacturer was cited for 14 observations documenting the organization's failure to properly review, approve (signatures), and/or date documentation when document changes occurred. Sometimes Dr. D thinks medical device companies hibernate and take refuge in a hibernaculum (look-up-time) versus living in the real world and addressing regulatory, quality, and compliance issues as they occur. **HELLO – 14 OBSERVATIONS ARE ABSURD.** Broken record time again – Dr. D emphatically states, "Having a quality system that complies with all aspects of the Quality System Regulation (QSR) is the basic cost of admission into the medical device industry." From Dr. D's perspective, if I notice a single occurrence during an audit, I typically treat the violation as an oversight and ask for immediate correction. Fourteen (14) observations is evidence of a complete system failure, or equally as bad, the complete absence of an effective system. Either way, you should be prepared to ask, "Where do I sign the Form 483?" In the case of this warning letter, there is an abundance of evidence supporting the lack of a documented procedure and subsequent process for effective document controls. I would have loved to see the look of shock on the investigator's face when he or she descried this organization's approach, or should I say lack of an approach, to document controls.

Warning Letter (March 2010)

> *Failure to establish and maintain procedures to control all documents that are required by 21 CFR Part 820, as required by 21 CFR 820.40. The procedures should designate an individual(s) to review for adequacy and approve prior to issuance all documents established to meet the requirements of 21 CFR Part 820. For example:*
>
> *a. When requested, no procedures which address document control were provided.*
> *b. The following unapproved documents are maintained in the Device History File, stored electronically, or are contract/(b)(4) agreements:*

1. The 3CPM Company, Inc. (b)(4) with no review or approval signatures.
2. The Design Plan entitled (b)(4) undated with no review or approval signatures.
3. SOP number (b)(4) no approval signature.
4. Document number (b)(4) undated with no approval signature.
5. Document number (b)(4) dated Ma 14, 2003 with no approval signature.
6. Test Report (b)(4) written by the firm's independent consultant, but not approved by 3CPM management
7. (b)(4) but does not have a review or approval signature.
8. (b)(4) but does not have a review or approval signature.
9. (b)(4) but does not have a review or approval signature.
10. (b)(4) undated with no approval signature
11. (b)(4) undated with no approval signature
12. (b)(4) undated with no approval signature
13. (b)(4) but updated.
14. "CONTRACT SERVICES AGREEMENT" between 3CPM Company, Inc (b)(4) undated with no signatures.

Quality System Regulation - 21 CFR, Part 820

QSR – Subpart D – Document Controls

Section 820.40 Document controls

Each manufacturer shall establish and maintain procedures to control all documents that are required by this part. The procedures shall provide for the following:

(a)*Document approval and distribution.* Each manufacturer shall designate an individual(s) to review for adequacy and approve prior to issuance all documents established to meet the requirements of this part. The approval, including the date and signature of the individual(s) approving the document, shall be documented. Documents established to meet the requirements of this part shall be available at all locations for which they are designated, used, or otherwise necessary, and all obsolete documents shall be promptly removed from all points of use or otherwise prevented from unintended use.

(b)*Document changes.* Changes to documents shall be reviewed and approved by an individual(s) in the same function or organization that performed the original review and approval, unless specifically designated otherwise. Approved changes shall be communicated to the appropriate personnel in a timely manner. Each manufacturer shall maintain records of changes to documents. Change records shall include a description of the change, identification of the affected documents, the signature of the approving individual(s), the approval date, and when the change becomes effective.

Document Controls

Let me begin by emphatically stating, "detailed written procedures are required that define the entire approach to document controls." Remember DG Rule # 6 – All procedures, work instructions, drawings, specifications, etc. must be written, well-documented, and controlled within a defined document control system. This applies to document controls, as well. Yes, to participate in the medical device industry we need to generate a whole bunch of procedures. Yes, we need to actually train and adhere to these procedures. Unfortunately, we also kill too many trees in pursuit of our need for procedures. For the record, electronic documentation is the only way to go – it is green and saves trees. Regardless, regulations, procedures, changes to regulations, changes to procedures, etc. is what keeps most of us quality and regulatory professionals gainfully employed.

Document Approval and Distribution (a)

In breaking down the regulation, you need to start by identifying the appropriate individuals that will be responsible for reviewing and approving documents prior to their release and subsequent use. For many organizations, this activity is performed as part of a Change Control Board (CCB) meeting. The same tasks can be accomplished electronically, with the current state-of-the-art of document-management systems. Either way, the intent of the regulation is to ensure qualified individuals are reviewing and approving documents prior to their release. Once again, the review and approval process requires a signature and the date reflecting the approval.

All documents, relevant to ongoing operations, must always be released and available for use at appropriate locations. For example, assembly instructions should be released to the manufacturing floor. In fact, all operators should always have the applicable assembly or work instruction available and opened at their workstation. Not to belabor a point, all inspection instructions should be available at the inspection stations, shipping and receiving procedures at the shipping and receiving workstations, etc. Are you following Dr. D's drift here? Additionally, all obsolete documentation must be quickly identified and removed from use. I recommend stamping each document with a **BOLD OBSOLETE STAMP** and quickly collecting each one. Since the expectation is that organizations know the exact quantity of documents issued, e.g. let us say seven (7) documents were previously issued; seven (7) documents need to be stamped as obsolete and collected when new revisions are released. Pretty simple concept, right?

Finally, although not specifically called out in this requirement, training is important. Every-single-time a change occurs to a procedure, work instruction, assembly instruction, inspection instruction, etc. the organization needs to ensure training to the new revision occurs. Trust Dr. D, the FDA will verify training is occurring to the new release of documents. If training is not occurring, can you say, "Where do I sign the Form 483?"

Document Changes (b)

Managing changes to documents requires the same diligence in regards to review, approval, and evidence of signatures and dates. When making changes to documents, ensure the same functional areas responsible for reviewing and approving the original document releases are included in the review and approval of subsequent changes. As with the previous section, ensure all changed documents, once approved, are quickly released for implementation and use; and do not forget to collect the obsolete documentation. As stated in the last section, adequate training to the changes must be pursued. Additionally, please ensure records of all changes are maintained. Once again, you will need to trust Dr. D as I inform you the FDA will review the change history of documents, when warranted, as part of their investigation. As a minimum, the following change request information is required:

1. A detailed description of the change;

2. A list of all documentation affected by the change;

3. The individual or organization requesting the change;

4. A list of change approvers;

5. The actual signature (can be electronic) and approval date of the change;

6. The effective date of the change; and

7. Additional information that may be relevant to supporting the change.

Takeaways for Chapter 7

In conclusion, medical device manufacturers need to focus on document controls. The control of documents is a cornerstone supporting the foundation for an effective quality system. It is imperative the latest and correct revisions of documentation, e.g., procedures, assembly instructions, inspection instructions, drawing, etc. are released and employed by medical device manufacturers. Additionally, all changes must receive the appropriate level of oversight in regards to reviews and approvals. Furthermore, similar to all records required in support of QSR compliance, signatures and dates are important. Finally, do not forget to identify and collect all documentation that has been identified as obsolete.

Chapter 8 – Purchasing Controls

21 CFR, Part 820

Subpart E

Section 820.50

Chapter 8 – Purchasing Controls

In this chapter, Dr. D will expand upon the virtues and the importance of effective processes for purchasing controls and supplier management, collectively. In fact, the FDA is really taking medical device manufacturers to task in regards to purchasing controls and the overall management of their suppliers. According to Kimberly Trautman, the FDA's current Good Manufacturing Practices (cGMP) and Quality System Regulations (QSR) expert, suppliers providing non-conforming material are directly related to an increase in medical device recalls; which increases the need for effective quality processes to mitigate risk. Remember, as the medical device industry continues to grow in leaps and bounds, industry experts are pullulating with ideas and approaches to effective purchasing controls and supplier management. Also remember, Dr. D., in the pursuit of apotheosis (look-it up time), will always travel the high road, and provide readers with an objective and common-sense approach to compliance.

FDA Warning Letter

I hope by now you have had a chance to visit the FDA's database depicting the issuance of warning letters by the agency. If you have, the first thing that you will notice is the significant increase in the number of letters the agency is issuing. If you have not, you do not know what you are missing. My goal, through the penning of Devine Guidance, is to ensure the organizations my readers support are not on the receiving end of an agency's love letter. In support of this chapter, the offending medical device manufacturer has failed to establish a policies and procedures for clearly defining the requirements for purchased products and services. Now granted, Dr. D. is not a polymer engineer or a resin expert; however, common sense should dictate the need for chemical and physical analysis of resins. Additionally, any type of change, regardless of the change

being rooted in material, process, maintenance procedure, etc. the entire process needs to

be documented and the results collected as evidence in support of compliance. That said,

the FDA, and rightly so, awarded this offending medical device manufacturer a warning

letter.

Warning Letter (February 2010)

Failure to establish and maintain data that clearly describes or references the specified requirements, including quality requirements, for purchased or otherwise received product and services, as required by 21 C.F.R. § 820.50(b). FDA 483 Item 4. Specifically:

a. Your firm has not requested from the foreign supplier certificates of analysis (COA) of the (b)(4) anion resin in order to verify that the received resin material conforms to the resin specifications or recognized AAMI standards for dialysis use. Your firm verbally stated that your supplier's sales representative kept the COA for you.

b. Your firm has not documented, approved, and maintained written specifications for the replacement carbon that was used to re-bed the carbon tanks, and the (b)(4) anion resin for the mixed-bed D1 tanks. Further, your firm verbally stated that you had changed the supplier of the carbon material in the last (2) years and had not documented a description of the change and approved the change.

Quality System Regulation - 21 CFR, Part 820

QSR – Subpart E – Purchasing Controls

Section 820.50 Purchasing controls

Each manufacturer shall establish and maintain procedures to ensure that all purchased or otherwise received product and services conform to specified requirements.

(a)Evaluation of suppliers, contractors, and consultants. Each manufacturer shall establish and maintain the requirements, including quality requirements, that must be met by suppliers, contractors, and consultants. Each manufacturer shall:

(1) Evaluate and select potential suppliers, contractors, and consultants on the basis of their ability to meet specified requirements, including quality requirements. The evaluation shall be documented.
(2) Define the type and extent of control to be exercised over the product, services, suppliers, contractors, and consultants, based on the evaluation results.
(3) Establish and maintain records of acceptable suppliers, contractors, and consultants.

(b)Purchasing data. Each manufacturer shall establish and maintain data that clearly describe or reference the specified requirements, including quality requirements, for purchased or otherwise received product and services. Purchasing documents shall include, where possible, an agreement that the suppliers, contractors, and consultants agree to notify the manufacturer of changes in the product or service so that manufacturers may determine whether the changes may affect the quality of a finished device. Purchasing data shall be approved in accordance with 820.40.

Purchasing Controls

Dr. D. will begin the analysis, for this chapter, with my customary broken record time. Broken record, "all of the requirements delineated within the QSR require written documentation that defines an organization's policies and procedures that reflect compliance." Remember DG Rule # 6 - All procedures, work instructions, drawings, specifications, etc. must be written, well-documented, and controlled within a defined document control system. Feel free to reread the doctor's guidance on document controls, as a refresher. That said, a procedure or series of procedures, which capture all aspects of the purchasing and supplier control functions needs to be created, including the extremely important Approved Supplier's List (ASL). Additionally, the intent of the requirement is to ensure procured products and services comply with requirements. Furthermore, your organization needs to define the requirements, in writing. Finally, the documented results, employed for determining if procured products or services reflect compliance with requirements, must be collected and retained. Remember, FDA visits are not audits, they are inspections; with the goal of collecting evidence if compliance to the QSR is not observed. Establishing well-defined requirements, and collecting and retaining objective data to support compliance to requirements, is the best defense during an FDA visit.

Evaluation of suppliers, contractors, and consultants (a)

The process for determining what constitutes an acceptable supplier, contractor, or consultant must be rooted in requirements. Guess who is tasked with setting these requirements? Yes, bingo – your organization needs to define the criteria for what is deemed an acceptable or qualified supplier. Dr. D recommends selecting suppliers that have approved EN ISO 13485 or ISO 9000 based quality systems from a recognized registrar or notified body. Will this piece of a paper, a.k.a. the quality system certificate equate to selecting a supplier capable of meeting requirements? Of course not; however, having an established and functioning quality system is half the battle.

Dr. D also recommends a system that places suppliers into categories premised on risk; (a) business, (b) product and (c) patient. The categories will define the amount of control needed for a supplier. For example, critical suppliers such as a sterilization facility or a component identified as critical during the execution of an FMEA should require an initial selection evaluation and probably an annual assessment. A supplier of floor-stock items such as fasteners may require only a mail-in assessment with an update once every two-years. A supplier of finger cots may require that only a current copy of their ISO quality system certificate is on file and retained. Regardless, your organization can exude some common sense and define the requirements. Additionally, Dr. D strongly recommends the assembly of a cross-functional team for an initial supplier assessment. The quality, purchasing, engineering, regulatory functions, etc. bring different insights and perspectives into the assessment process. A 360-degree approach to on-site assessments, supported by a cross-function team, will improve the overall effectiveness of the supplier selection and evaluation process.

When defining requirements, you need to ensure that a path for disqualifying suppliers is also available. In fact, the selection criteria should contain sufficient granularity that supplier approval categories; e.g., approved, not approved approval pending, probation, or disqualified are delineated. Additionally, supplier requirements will vary depending upon the commodity or service being procured. Supplier-specific requirements must be accounted for as part of defining overall supplier requirements. For example, a supplier of polymers or resins will have different requirements that that of a precision-machining facility. Furthermore, any special supplier requirements must be defined. Dr. D. recommends creating a supplier agreement for complex relationships that clearly define the roles and responsibilities of the supplier, as well as the procuring organization. Finally, everything associated with purchasing controls and the entire supplier-management process shall be documented. Remember DG Rule # 3 - Document the results of all events in writing, because if it is not documented in writing, the event did not occur.

Purchasing Data (b)

In the context of the QSR, purchasing data is the creation and collection of all of the documentation needed to accurately define the policies, procedures, requirements, specifications, etc. employed in the procurement of product and services for the medical device industry. It is the hope of Dr. D. that as a minimum, purchase orders are being issued to suppliers, which define with sufficient granularity, the requirements for the products or services being procured. This includes contractors and consultants. Additionally, the FDA recommends the use of agreements with suppliers that clearly delineate a policy for change notification. It is Dr. D's recommendation that a zero change or "no-change" policy be pursued. Remember any change that influences the finished medical device, product packaging, or product labeling needs to be evaluated and probably revalidated, when changes occur. Depending on the product classification, a formal review and approval by the FDA, e.g. PMA supplement, may be required prior to implementing proposed changes. Finally, all data must be reviewed, approved, and maintained in accordance with the regulation's requirement for document controls.

Takeaways for Chapter 8

As for Chapter 8, the key takeaways are:

1. Establish well-defined procedures for purchasing controls;

2. Create an accurate ASL and maintain it accordingly;

3. Establish categories for your suppliers premised on risk;

4. Once categories are established audit your suppliers per a predefined schedule and more frequently if issues arise;

5. When possible, employ cross-function teams during audits;

6. Use supplier agreements as a tool for managing business relationships;

7. Ensure an avenue that clearly defines a process for proposed supplier changes exists;

8. Dr. D. strongly recommends a no-change policy as revalidation efforts can be expensive; and

9. All records associated with purchasing controls must be retained, sustained, maintained, and available to the agency so you will not be entertained when they issue a Form 483, for failure to comply.

Remember, evidence of compliance is always an organization's best defense when the FDA shows up on your doorstep for a friendly visit.

Chapter 9 – Identification and Traceability

21 CFR, Part 820

Subpart F

Sections 820.60 and 820.65

Chapter 9 – Identification and Traceability

The identification and traceability (sections 820.60 and 820.65) for products and finished medical devices, throughout the entire manufacturing process, including raw materials employed during the manufacturing process, and the subsequent sale and distribution of medical devices, are critical elements of the Quality System Regulation (QSR). In fact, maintaining batch control and if required, serial number control for specific medical devices are salient requirements of the regulation. Why? Because when the safety and efficacy of a finished medical device comes into question, medical device manufacturers must be able to quickly identify and recover the devices. Yes, Dr. D despises that dirty little word **RECALL.** However, a recall is inevitable in this business, as the mighty Mr. Murphy is always lurking in some corner. Additionally, without the ability to determine root cause either to a specific component failure, batch of components, raw material lot, or batch of finished medical devices, recalls can result in a substantial number of devices being withdrawn from market. Remember, recalls are expensive so effective identification and traceability can limit the fiscal exposure. Having said that, creating a rock-solid system for identification and traceability is always in the best interest of medical device manufacturers or as Dr. D would like to state; "a pay me now versus pay me later scenario." Dr. D would never want to be that obstreperous (look-it-up time) quality or regulatory specialist having to explain a non-compliant approach for identification and traceability to the agency.

FDA Warning Letter

It took Dr. D a considerable amount of time to find an offender in support of this chapter. Exactly why, the good doctor is not sure so I will let you draw your own conclusions. The way Dr. D views this lack of observations noted by the FDA are rooted in two possible outcomes. In the first scenario, just about all medical device manufacturers understand the importance of identification and traceability and willingly comply with the requirement, e.g., medical device manufacturing Valhalla. In scenario two, the FDA is just not spending much time on this specific requirement because they are having too much fun issuing Form 483s and warning letters for the more egregious violations associated with design controls, process controls, and purchasing controls. Regardless of the reason, the outcome is in actuality self-evident; compliance to all of the requirements, delineated within the QSR, is mandatory. The offending party on the receiving end of this warning letter, lacked procedures and processes for all aspects of product identification, throughout all stages of production. On a very sad note, this was the 10th observation depicted in a very lengthy warning letter.

Warning Letter (March 2009)

> *10. Your firm has not established and maintained procedures for identifying product throughout all stages of receipt, production, packaging, distribution, and installation to prevent mix-ups, as required by 21 C.F.R. § 820.60.*
> *10A: Your firm has no written procedures for incoming receipt and acceptance of raw materials. Your firm lacks traceability as to specific shipments of raw material used in product and testing of each lot of finished devices. No internal lot number or other control number is assigned to clearly differentiate each shipment of material received from other shipments, and supplier lot numbers are not recorded.*
>
> *10B: Part numbers recorded on the work instruction forms for the raw material goat anti-mouse antibody and the Reagent Solution produced from that raw material were noted to be the same.*
>
> *The lot number of the manufacturer's raw material is used by the firm as its production lot number. Further, the firm uses the same manufacturer's lot number for the raw material goat anti-mouse antibody to produce different concentrations of the Reagent Solution for Control Line, and continues to assign the same lot number to each batch of finished Reagent Solution for Control Line produced. In sum, unique lot and part numbers are not assigned in order to prevent mix-ups.*

10C: Laminated sheets were observed to lack any product identification whatsoever. Among other things, without a system to uniquely identify and clearly distinguish in-process materials, the incorrect material could be used in manufacturing resulting in production of a finished device which does not meet specifications.

Quality System Regulation - 21 CFR, Part 820

QSR – Subpart F – Identification & Traceability

Section 820.60 Identification

Each manufacturer shall establish and maintain procedures for identifying product during all stages of receipt, production, distribution, and installation to prevent mixups.

Section 820.65 Traceability

Each manufacturer of a device that is intended for surgical implant into the body or to support or sustain life and whose failure to perform when properly used in accordance with instructions for use provided in the labeling can be reasonably expected to result in a significant injury to the user shall establish and maintain procedures for identifying with a control number each unit, lot, or batch of finished devices and where appropriate components. The procedures shall facilitate corrective action. Such identification shall be documented in the DHR.

Identification and Traceability

They key to an effective system for identification and traceability is a well-defined approach to Material Requirements Planning (MRP) / Enterprise Resource Planning (ERP). My assumption is that all medical device manufacturers pursue an automated approach to MRP / ERP through the employment of SAP™, QAD™, or similar systems. The architecture of these systems supports the batch management of raw materials, components, chemicals, manufactured subassemblies and finished medical devices. Additionally, most MRP / ERP platforms contain functionality in regards to assigning specific serial numbers, when required. Furthermore, regardless of the approach to MRP / ERP, medical device manufactures must be able to retain accurate records in regards to product shipments to specific customers. Accurate records will be needed to facilitate a timely and organized recovery of medical devices should a **RECALL** become necessary.

Identification

The identification requirement of the QSR is not what Dr. D would categorize as a requirement rooted in rocket science. For starters (broken record time), medical device manufacturers must write and maintain procedures covering all functional areas and aspects of their business, including identification and traceability. The procedures must support claims of compliance to the e QSR. Trust Dr. D when I say, "the FDA will issue a Form 483 if procedures employed to support compliance with the regulations are absent or lack depth and clarity." Remember DG Rule # 6 – All procedures, work instructions, drawings, specifications, etc. must be written, well-documented, and controlled with in a defined document control system."

In support of the identification requirement, a few takeaways for compliance are depicted in the following six-bulleted points.

1. Treat batch management as a mandatory requirement for raw materials, components, products, chemicals, etc. employed as part of the manufacturing process. A safe rule of thumb to pursue is that any procured item influencing the product (finished medical device), the packaging (finished medical device), or the labeling (product label, package label, Instructions for Use), should be controlled through a batch management system

2. For age-sensitive material, storage conditions and expiration dates are critical to ensure service life is not exceeded. It is an important feature of any MRP system

to be able to track and manage expiration dates. This holds true for finished devices as well.

3. During production, batch management is equally important. Dr. D strongly recommends pursuing a robust line-clearance approach to prevent material and batch mixing during the manufacturing process. This includes the ability to segregate and quickly quarantine non-conforming products.

4. Batch management and potentially serial number management is required to comply with the requirement. Additionally, the Device History Record (DHR) is the receptacle for the complete batch history of finished medical device(s) and must be retained as evidence of compliance to the regulation. Once again, you need to trust Dr. D as I emphatically state; "the agency will examine DHRs during their friendly visits." Furthermore, if the visit is "for cause" because of a specific field action, aka, **RECALL**, the agency could spend days and potentially weeks examining DHRs, so a significant amount of effort must be exuded when compiling each DHR with evidence of strict adherence with the identification requirement, collectively.

5. Identification is also required for "installation" and implies capital equipment must be clearly identified under the regulation. For example, a medical device manufacturer that manufactures radio-frequency (RF) ablation catheters may also sell the capital equipment, or in this example, an RF generator to support the disposable business. The manufacturer, as part of the installation process, is responsible for the identification of the RF generator. The piece of capital

equipment should have a unique serial number and the manufacturer should compile and retain a DHR. If subsequent upgrades, firmware changes, software changes, etc. are made, the manufacturer is not only tasked with incorporating the changes but ensuring the DHR captures all of the changes for a specific piece of capital equipment. Trust Dr. D when I say; "batch management of medical devices is a challenging task; however, management of capital equipment identification is down-right daunting.

6. When in doubt, always invoke identification through the employment of batch control. An organization can always remove the requirement if it is determined batch control, for a specific item e.g., finger cots, is not required.

Traceability

Similar to identification, Dr. D is going to invoke the not rocket science clause as the requirement for traceability is rooted in common sense. The requirement begins with clear pointers to the device: (a) being deployed as a surgical implant (placed into the body); (b) used to support or sustain life when properly (safety and efficacy) used (hopefully employed in a procedure by a trained and licensed physician); and (c) failure of the device to perform in accordance with the instructions for use (product labeling), which results in ***significant*** injury. If the manufactured medical device meets the criteria depicted in the previous sentence, the manufacturer better make damn sure the appropriate policies and procedures are in place to ensure the device has a batch number, lot number, serial number, control number or any number deemed appropriate to track the device back to its manufacturing roots. What Dr. D, back to the manufacturing roots? In short, traceability needs to be captured in the DHR. Additionally, traceability needs to be back to the component level and when deemed appropriate, all the way back to the supplier. Furthermore, the device traceability needs to be robust enough to be able to support corrective actions, up to and including a **RECALL**.

Takeaways from Chapter 9

The salient points from Chapter 9 are: (a) a written procedure(s) describing identification and traceability is/are mandatory; and (b) place an emphasis on effective batch and if warranted, serial-number control. Additionally, the procedure(s) should focus on specific requirements identified for traceability:

1. Product being deployed as a surgical implant (placed into the body);

2. Product utilized to support or sustain life when properly (safety and efficacy) used (hopefully employed in a procedure by a trained and licensed physician); and

3. Failure for the device to perform in accordance with the instructions for use (product labeling).

Chapter 10 – Production and Process Controls

21 CFR, Part 820

Subpart G

Section 820.70

Chapter 10 – Production and Process Controls

The Quality System Regulation (QSR), for production and process controls, (21 CFR, Part 820 – Subpart G, Section 820.70) is in the opinion of Dr. D one of the more salient requirements of the regulation. In fact, the FDA has frequently focused their efforts on production and process controls during their friendly visits. If you have any reservations in regards to the agency's resolve, I recommend a quick trip to the FDA's website; specifically, enforcement actions and look at the number of warning letters issued for the lack of or ineffective production and process controls. Similar to design control, the requirements for production and process controls are substantial. Remember, compliance is the key (broken-record time), compliance is the key; (again) and compliance is the key to success in this industry, along designing and manufacturing a medical device that is safe and effective.

Additionally, buildings and equipment fall into Dr. D's not rocket science category. Why? Because the investments made, by medical device manufacturers, into buildings and equipment, are in reality a down payment toward the price of admission into the medical device industry. Besides, ask your district office of the FDA if assembling a Class 3 device, for arguments sake an electrophysiological catheter; (a) in your backyard, (b) using tools just purchased from the Home Depot or Lowes, (c) while wearing cargo shorts and flip-flops, is an acceptable practice. Be prepared to step aside and listen to the hysterical laughter emanating from the district office. All kidding aside, the expectation is that a suitable facility, with equipment and tooling that has been verified, validated, calibrated, etc., be employed in the manufacturing of devices. A medical device manufacturer's nescience (look-it-up) in regards to the quality systems regulation (QSR) will be rewarded, with a Form 483, and potentially a warning letter; if the violations are bountiful and egregious to these specific requirements, and the QSR, as a whole.

Furthermore, compliance issues, associated with automated processes, have emerged onto the agency's radar screen. There are growing numbers of warning letters and Form 483 observations that reflect enforcement trends in regards to this requirement. Specifically, software and the need to control and validate software employed as part of the manufacturing process. In short, relying on the "it is just a black box" is no longer a valid defense. The agency wants to ensure all automated processes are documented and validated.

Finally, if your organization does not want to be on the receiving end of a congeries (look-it-up if you need to) of Form 483 observations, during one of the FDA friendly visits, Dr. D strongly recommends compliance to 820.70; and all of the other requirements delineated within the QSR

FDA Warning Letter One

It took Dr. D all but a New York minute; or is it a New York second, to find offending parties for this chapter of the book. As you will quickly be able to ascertain, after reading the excerpts from the warning letter, the FDA was thoroughly impressed with this organization's approach to production and process control, or should I say lack of an approach. In fact, the FDA was equally impressed with the initial Form 483 responses put forth by this medical device manufacturer. Yes, I know – enough of the sarcasm Dr. D.

Warning Letter One (May 2010)

Observation One (1)

> 3. Production processes were not adequately developed, conducted, controlled, and monitored to ensure that devices conform to their specifications. 21 CPR §820.70(a). Specifically, you have failed to adequately develop, monitor, and control production processes in order to ensure reliability and repeatability of the manufacturing process. For example:
>
> > A) Your firm's procedure for testing the quality of your water (SOP 036, Revision F) which is used to process products requires root cause investigations and re-testing to be performed immediately for water samples that fail action limits. On December 24, 2009, your contract laboratory reported to you that the conductivity test result (198 uS at 25 degrees Celsius) for port 10 did not conform to specifications. Your firm failed to perform a retest or investigate the OOS result as per your written procedure.
> >
> > B) Your firm's Routine Product Bioburden Testing SOP 046, Revision B. describes random sampling (b)(4). However, your firm has no documentation to show that (b)(4) final samples were taken from a (b)(4) manufacturing technician during the January 11, 2008, July 15, 2008, and July 31, 2009 bioburden testing as required by your written procedure.
> >
> > C) Your Routine Product Bioburden Testing SOP 046, Revision B, specifies increased limits when compared to your 2008 and 2009 quarterly Artegraft product bioburden test results. There was no scientific data provided during the inspection to demonstrate the appropriateness for the limits set in your written procedure

FDA Response to Observation One (1).

> We have reviewed your response pertaining to FDA-483 observation 5 (A2, B, C) and have concluded that your response was not adequate because of the following:
>
> > a) Your response does not provide any evidence that the failing water results for port 10 were erroneous. Your firm has failed to follow your own written procedure which requires root cause investigations and re-testing to be performed immediately for water samples that fail action limits. It is your responsibility to ensure that manufacturing processes remain in a state of control in order to produce devices that conform to their specifications.
> >
> > b) No evidence of training was provided to show implementation of routine sampling which would include quarterly bioburden samples to be submitted per operator.
> >
> > c) No evidence was provided in your response to support your new alert and action limits for bioburden.

Observation Two (2)

> 4. Failure to establish and maintain adequate procedures to control environmental conditions that could reasonably be expected to have an adverse effect on product quality and failure to periodically inspect environmental control systems to verify that the system is adequate and functioning properly. 21 CFR§ 820.70(c). For example:
>
> > A) Your firm's "Environmental Monitoring, Sampling and Corrective Action for the manufacturing Facility and Personnel", Revision H, does not require your firm to monitor the positive pressure even though your validation report for Artegraft's

*manufacturing facility, dated May 3, 1999, requires positive pressurization in **(b)(4)** from the **(b)(4)** and to **(b)(4)**.*

B) Your firm's "Environmental Monitoring, Sampling and Corrective Action for the manufacturing Facility and Personnel", Revision, H, requires swab sampling of the Artegraft and D-Clot manufacturing rooms and personnel sampling to determine the microbial burden within the manufacturing , environment and on the operator's gloves. However, at the time of this inspection no alert and action limits had been established by your firm for swab sampling and personnel sampling.

C) Your firm's "Environmental Monitoring, Sampling and Corrective Action for the Manufacturing Facility and Personnel", Revision H, requires trend analysis to be performed on all resultant data in order to determine increases in all areas for microbial and non-viable particulate activity. However, at the time of this inspection no trend analysis was performed by your firm.

FDA Response to Observation Two (2)

We have reviewed your response pertaining to FDA-483 observation 5 (A2, B, C) and have concluded that your response was not adequate because of the following:

a) No evidence was provided to support that you will be able to adequately monitor continuous positive pressure in your Artegraft manufacturing facility (Requirement per your Artegraft's manufacturing validation report). Manufacturers are required to establish and maintain adequate procedures to control environmental conditions that could reasonably be expected to have an adverse effect on product quality. As a part of the requirement, manufacturers are required to periodically inspect environmental control systems to verify that the system, including necessary equipment, is adequate and functioning properly and these activities are documented and reviewed.

b) No evidence was provided in your response to support your alert and action limits for swab sampling and personnel sampling.

c) No evidence of training was provided in your response to support implementation of your QA Data Trending and Analysis (SOP 51) procedure.

Observation Three (3)

*5. Failure to ensure that all equipment used in the manufacturing process meets specified requirements and is appropriately designed, constructed, placed, and installed to facilitate maintenance, adjustment, cleaning, and use. 21 CFR § 820.70(g). Specifically, your firm failed to provide the FDA investigator with procedures for inspecting, monitoring, and maintaining a **(b)(4)** Refrigerator, ID # 00059, that is used for the temporary storage of raw materials and in-process vascular graft materials used for manufacturing.*

FDA Response to Observation Three (3)

We have reviewed your response pertaining to FDA-483 observation 7 and have concluded that your response was not adequate because of the following:

*a) Your proposed written procedure for transporting grafts in and out of the **(b)(4)** refrigerator, WI-MFG-011, Revision A, is not adequate since this procedure does not require maintenance schedules for the adjustment, cleaning, and other maintenance of your refrigerator in order to ensure that manufacturing* *specifications are met. Manufacturers must also conduct periodic inspections in accordance with established procedures to ensure adherence to applicable equipment maintenance schedules. When maintenance activity is required, the manufacturer must document and follow procedures for inspection of maintenance activities to ensure that such activity is conducted according to schedule, that all activities have been completed, and that equipment specification requirements continue to be met.*

b) Your firm must ensure that all equipment that is used in manufacturing meets specified requirements and it must be appropriately designed, constructed, placed, and installed to facilitate maintenance, adjustment, cleaning, and use. Your response does not provide us with any evidence that the (b)(4) refrigerator is suitable for the temporary storage of raw materials and in-process vascular graft materials which are used for manufacturing products. By not adequately maintaining and inspecting the refrigerator, products that do not meet specifications may be used in the manufacture of the devices, which could ultimately lead to the finished devices not meeting specifications.

FDA Warning Letter Two

Identifying an offender of 820.70, from the FDA's enforcement website, continues to be child's play. FDA noted violations of this requirement are frequent. Additionally, most violations are rooted in the lack of procedures or adequate procedures reflecting compliance to the requirements for production and process controls. Furthermore, compliance to my frequently quoted DG Rule # 6; "All procedures, work instructions, drawings, specifications, etc. must be written, well-documented, and controlled within a defined document control system," would result in a significant reduction in Form 483 observations and subsequent warning letters issued by the agency. Moreover, responding correctly and fully to Form 483 observations can save an organization from the pain of receiving a warning letter, and the business interruptions that accompany these enforcement actions. Can you say interruption of new product approvals? Finally, if you really want to endear your organization to the FDA, fell free to partake in the practice of repeat observations, similar to this offender's effort.

Warning Letter Two (May 2010)

Observation One (1) 12 observations

> *8. Failure to establish and maintain adequate procedures to prevent contamination of equipment or product by substances that could reasonably be expected to have an adverse effect on product quality, as required by 21 CFR 820.70(e). This is a repeat observation from the previous FDA 483 issued on 11/20/07. For example, your procedure for cleaning and maintenance of the manufacturing areas (Q53-P03, Revision 02) did not identify a schedule for routine cleaning of air vents in the dry room areas where product is assembled. During the inspection on 1/13/10 the vents were covered in dust and debris in Dry Room#(b)(4)*

FDA's Response to Observation One (1)

> *We have reviewed your response and concluded that it is not adequate because although you stated that a procedure was written to define and schedule air vent cleaning, you did not state if the air vents would be immediately cleaned or provided the written procedure for FDA's review.*

Observation Two (2)

> *11. Failure to establish and maintain procedures to adequately control environmental conditions that could reasonably be expected to have an adverse effect on product quality, as required by CFR 21 820.70(c). This is a repeat observation from FDA 483 issued on 11/20/2007. For example, the firm does not have temperature and humidity controls in the VirTis Lyophilizer Room, Room &(b)(4) where mini-batch lots are stored and require controlled temperature and humidity conditions.*

FDA's Response to Observation Two (2)

> *Your response to this observation appears to be adequate.*

FDA Warning Letter Three

This violator of the QSR was attempting to try for an agency record. In fact, the warning letter retrieved depicted 19-observations, documenting significant violations of the QSR. **What - are you kidding me?** Nineteen (19) observations, noted in the warning letter, are completely unacceptable. Can you say out-of-control? In fact, if Dr. D counted all of the subsections to these observations, and additional thirty-four (34) non-conformances were noted, expanding the grand total to fifty-three (53) observations identified. Yes, Dr. D possesses some basic mathematic skills, the doctor can add. **Are**

you kidding me? Fifty-three notations for compliance issues – you have to be kidding. If Dr. D were the recipient of this warning letter, my two-biggest concerns, after I have provided an initial response to the agency, would be; (1) when are the doors to the facility going to be chained and locked, and (2) will I look good in an orange jumpsuit?

Warning Letter Three (March 2010)

> *Observation* **9 of 19**. Failure to validate computer software for its intended use according to an established protocol when computers or automated data processing systems are used as part of production or the quality system, as required by 21 CFR 820.70(i). For example, when requested no validation documentation to support the commercial off-the-shelf program **(b)(4)** used to capture complaints, returned merchandise and service requests was provided.

FDA Warning Letter Four

This warning-letter recipient failed to validate software used in computers and data systems, employed to manage their businesses. The observations appear to be relatively benign because the findings incriminate report generation employed as part of management meetings; and the employment of commercial-off-the-shelf (COTS) software. However, the QSR explicitly states; "*When computers or automated data processing systems are used as part of production or the quality system, the manufacturer shall validate computer software for its intended use according to an established protocol.*" Although Dr. D is not a software guru, I recommend that all device manufacturers also become fluent in 21 CFR, Part 11 in support of understanding the agency's overall compliance direction in regards to software, changes to software, instrumentation inputs and outputs, which are all germane to achieving and sustaining compliance with the QSR. Remember, electronic signatures and records are important too.

Warning Letter Four (February 2010)

Observation 3 of 7. *Failure to validate computer software for its intended use according to an established protocol when computers or automated data processing systems are used as part of production or the quality system, as required by 21 C.F.R. §820.70(i) (Production and Process Controls - Automated Processes). For example, the CAPA analysis of nonconformances, which is used at management meetings, is inadequate in that the report is computer-generated on a non-validated software system.*

FDA Response to Observation 3 of 7. *We have reviewed your response and have concluded that it is inadequate because you state that you have eliminated the electronic recordkeeping for CAPA. but you have not provided evidence of an adequate recordkeeping system to replace the electronic system.*

Quality System Regulation - 21 CFR, Part 820

QSR – Subpart G – Production and Process Controls

Section 820.70

(a)General. Each manufacturer shall develop, conduct, control, and monitor production processes to ensure that a device conforms to its specifications. Where deviations from device specifications could occur as a result of the manufacturing process, the manufacturer shall establish and maintain process control procedures that describe any process controls necessary to ensure conformance to specifications. Where process controls are needed they shall include:
    (1) Documented instructions, standard operating procedures (SOP's), and methods that define and control the manner of production;
    (2) Monitoring and control of process parameters and component and device characteristics during production;
    (3) Compliance with specified reference standards or codes;
    (4) The approval of processes and process equipment; and
    (5) Criteria for workmanship which shall be expressed in documented standards or by means of identified and approved representative samples.

(b)Production and process changes. Each manufacturer shall establish and maintain procedures for changes to a specification, method, process, or procedure. Such changes shall be verified or where appropriate validated according to 820.75, before implementation and these activities shall be documented. Changes shall be approved in accordance with 820.40.

(c)Environmental control. Where environmental conditions could reasonably be expected to have an adverse effect on product quality, the manufacturer shall establish and maintain procedures to adequately control these environmental conditions. Environmental control system(s) shall be periodically inspected to verify that the system, including necessary equipment, is adequate and functioning properly. These activities shall be documented and reviewed.

(d)Personnel. Each manufacturer shall establish and maintain requirements for the

health, cleanliness, personal practices, and clothing of personnel if contact between such personnel and product or environment could reasonably be expected to have an adverse effect on product quality. The manufacturer shall ensure that maintenance and other personnel who are required to work temporarily under special environmental conditions are appropriately trained or supervised by a trained individual.

(e)Contamination control. Each manufacturer shall establish and maintain procedures to prevent contamination of equipment or product by substances that could reasonably be expected to have an adverse effect on product quality.

(f)Buildings. Buildings shall be of suitable design and contain sufficient space to perform necessary operations, prevent mixups, and assure orderly handling.

(g)Equipment. Each manufacturer shall ensure that all equipment used in the manufacturing process meets specified requirements and is appropriately designed, constructed, placed, and installed to facilitate maintenance, adjustment, cleaning, and use.

(1)Maintenance schedule. Each manufacturer shall establish and maintain schedules for the adjustment, cleaning, and other maintenance of equipment to ensure that manufacturing specifications are met. Maintenance activities, including the date and individual(s) performing the maintenance activities, shall be documented.

(2)Inspection. Each manufacturer shall conduct periodic inspections in accordance with established procedures to ensure adherence to applicable equipment maintenance schedules. The inspections, including the date and individual(s) conducting the inspections, shall be documented.

(3)Adjustment. Each manufacturer shall ensure that any inherent limitations or allowable tolerances are visibly posted on or near equipment requiring periodic adjustments or are readily available to personnel performing these adjustments.

(h)Manufacturing material. Where a manufacturing material could reasonably be expected to have an adverse effect on product quality, the manufacturer shall establish and maintain procedures for the use and removal of such manufacturing material to ensure that it is removed or limited to an amount that does not adversely affect the device's quality. The removal or reduction of such manufacturing material shall be documented.

(i)Automated processes. When computers or automated data processing systems are used as part of production or the quality system, the manufacturer shall validate computer software for its intended use according to an established protocol. All software changes shall be validated before approval and issuance. These validation activities and results shall be documented.

Production and Process Controls

Production and process controls, in the opinion of Dr. D., is where the proverbial "rubber meets the road," in support of medical device manufacturing. All aspects of the manufacturing process, for medical device manufacturers, should be detailed in the processes and procedures employed. Additionally, conformance to defined specifications is an important takeaway. Furthermore, the QSR is very specific and states; "Each manufacturer shall develop, conduct, control, and monitor production processes to ensure that a device conforms to its specifications." Finally, remember there are serious ramifications for the failure of manufactured medical devices to meet their specifications or function in their intended use. Can you say **RECALL?**

(a) General

Broken record time – adherence to Dr. D's Rule # 6 – All procedures, work instructions, drawings, specifications, etc. must be written, well-documented, and controlled within a defined document control system, is required.

(1) The path towards compliance begins with well-written procedures, manufacturing work instructions and quality inspection instructions in support of production. Remember, no matter how benign a manufacturing step, inspection step, or process, might appear to be, ensuring work or inspection instructions clearly spell out the steps and expected outcomes is mission critical. The word that comes to mind should be "*precise*."

(2) Process and device performance characteristics need to be **<u>continuously</u> <u>monitored</u>** throughout the entire manufacturing process. Additionally, test results and inspection results should be documented and the results retained in the Device History Record (DHR). Furthermore, if warranted, special processes or critical processes that require special set-ups may require ongoing monitoring as part of the production environment. For example, tensile testing, ultrasonic welding, or similar processes may

require special or precise setups and a set-up sheet or log book, for tracking process performance, while ensuring such critical processes remain in control. As depicted in the first warning letter extraction in this chapter, bioburden just might be a good process to focus on, as the agency sure did. Do not forget about monitoring external processes as well, e.g., sterilization or even critical processes being executed by suppliers. All processes, regardless of the controls being internal or external, need to be evaluated and monitored. Finally, Dr. D recommends the employment of Statistical Process Control (SPC) wherever possible. The assignment of some level of process capability, a.k.a., Ppk, is always a valuable production tool employed for gauging process effectiveness. Can you say Six Sigma?

One important, no very important, no extremely important takeaway for production and process controls is the verification and validation of all manufacturing processes, including test methods. Dr. D. will cover Section 820.75, process validation in the next chapter.

(3) Compliance with specified reference standards or codes means compliance to FDA mandated standards or internally developed and validated standards may not be sufficient. The selection and application of appropriate standards must be all-encompassing. What in the heck does that mean Dr. D? For example, ISTA-2A may be a necessary standard to ensure product is packaged and protected while ensuring the manufactured medical device is delivered to the healthcare provider, through normal distribution stressors, undamaged. ISTA is the acronym for the International Safe Transit Association; and their standards are recognized as supporting compliance with EN ISO 11607-1 & -2. Other external standards such as those created by the Association for the

Advancement of Medical Instrumentation (AAMI) may be required, depending upon the products being manufactured. Compliance to external codes is also a mandated requirement. For example, Proposition 65 (California) requires companies operating within the state or introducing products for commerce into the state to comply with requirements of the statute. Proposition 65 delineates specific requirements for the handling and disposal of toxic chemicals, the posting of warning – e.g., "carcinogen – may cause cancer in quality professionals and FDA investigators" (just kidding about the quality professionals), or the requirement for specific labeling requirements when chemicals, and materials – e.g., DEHP, are employed as part of the manufacturing process or inherent in the finished medical device.

(4) Employing approved processes and equipment (do not forget about software) for the manufacture of medical devices, are fundamental requirements for medical device manufacturers. As I stated earlier, process validation will be covered in the next chapter. That being said, **ALL PROCESSES** employed in the manufacture of medical devices require validation. Additionally, the expectation is that all equipment employed in the manufacture of medical devices be submitted to Installation Qualification (IQ), Operational Qualification (OQ), and Performance Qualification (PQ). Furthermore, all equipment employed as part of the manufacturing process should be calibrated, if warranted , and placed into a preventive maintenance program, as necessary. Just a friendly reminder from Dr. D, please ensure all manufacturing personnel are trained to approved and released processes and the operators are trained to verify the operational status of manufacturing equipment, including the calibration status. Finally, broken record time again – **All training shall be documented!**

(5) If your organization employs workmanship standards, ensure the standards are documented and released within your document control system. Manufacturing and quality personnel should be trained to the workmanship standards and just like the previous section, training must be documented. Additionally, your organization may select the use of samples to be employed as part of the workmanship standard. In fact, Dr. D loves the use of samples for inspection applications, providing the samples are controlled, and the samples are themselves evaluated and maintained as part of the equipment preventive maintenance and calibration system. In short, you do not want to employ samples that have the potential for significant degradation, over time.

(b) Production and Process Changes

Feel free to make all of the production and process changes that you want. The agency no longer cares about medical device manufacturers making changes. **WHAT?** Just kidding, Dr. D just wants to ensure I still have your attention. Changes to production or processes, regardless of how benign such changes appear, need to be assessed. For Class 1 and Class 2 products, e.g., 510(k), in the United States, the proverbial letter-to-file, should suffice. However, for Class 3 devices (PMA), a 30-day PMA Supplement may be in order, depending upon the changes. If the change to production or process is significant such as moving a product line, a 180-day review by the agency may be required. When in doubt, contact the FDA and ask. Regardless of the changes, verification and validation activities need to be pursued; and remember all changes need to be documented, reviewed, and approved, by the appropriate levels of oversight and authority (remember Section 820.40). Finally, if production and process changes are not managed in accordance with the regulation, let Dr. D refresh your memory with the extremely scary 6-letter word – **RECALL!** Rest assured, the agency can and will quickly ascertain if serious compliance issues exist; and begin issuing the famous Form 483, documenting observations of non-compliance, as a reward. Depending on the egregiousness of the violation or the quantity of violations noted, organizations may receive additional recognition, **a warning letter!**

(c) Environmental Control

For starters, environmental control is much more than ensuring work surfaces are clean, the production floor swept, and the manufacturing area sustained at a comfortable 72-degrees Fahrenheit. Believe it or not, the FDA requires effective environmental controls that have been documented in a procedure. Surprised? Additionally, employees and contractors, including the janitorial staff need to be trained to the environmental control procedure(s). Surprised? Furthermore, the training shall be documented. Surprised? Finally, if your organization lacks procedures, training, and records of training in support of environmental control, or any QSR requirement, the FDA will issue a Form 483, which should not be a surprise. If compliance transgressions are deemed egregious, the look of surprise, on the faces of the management team, as they read the warning letter, will probably be priceless; and no – Dr. D does not like surprises.

Therefore, what does the FDA expect in regards to environmental control? In actuality, the agency would like to see a Class 1000 clean room in accordance with FED-STD-209 (just kidding). The regulation requires that the manufacturing environment be appropriate for the medical devices being manufactured. For example, manufacturing non-sterile devices or assembling pieces of capital equipment may warrant a reduced level of controlled environment, i.e., a clean work environment, manufacturing floor maintained at room temperature, with operators wearing lab coats. Manufacturing sterile devices such as catheters will probably require a controlled environment equal to or potentially better than a Class 10,000 environment, along with all of the trimming. If your organization is manufacturing implantable devices, the Class 1000 crack made in the previous paragraph may not be too far from the truth. The decision as to the required level of environment control is up to the device manufacturer; however, be prepared to defend your rationale.

For medical device manufacturers, a controlled environment is required for assembling medical devices. Wow - real rocket science right Dr. D. Some of the requirements that should be considered when writing the procedure and establishing the controlled environment are:

1. No food or drink consumption (pizza & beer is ok – just kidding);

2. No smoking or chewing of tobacco, gum, etc.;

3. A well-maintained HVAC system (including calibration), with High Efficiency Particulate Air (HEPA) Filtration capable of maintaining positive pressure, reduced particulate (<10,000 parts-per-million), while sustaining stable temperature and humidity;

4. A gowning procedure for all personnel entering the controlled environment;

5. Gowns, hair nets, beard and moustache covers, booties;

6. Detailed work instructions for cleaning all work areas;

7. The 24/7 monitoring of temperature and humidity, employing **calibrated chart recorders**;

8. Controlled pass-through areas for moving material into and out of the controlled

environment;

9. The infamous sticky mats at the entrance of the controlled environment;

10. Hot water and soap capable of removing layers of skin (just kidding);

11. Laminar flow hoods, when warranted for specific work areas;

12. Non-particulate generating wipes, finger cots, gloves, etc.; and finally,

13. Broken record time – all activities documented and reviewed. Remember DG

    Rule # 3 - Document the results of all events in writing, because if it is not

    documented in writing, the events did not occur.

Remember, you will need to validate the controlled environment prior to its use. You will

also have to sustain the environment 24/7; and have records available to prove

compliance to the agency.

(d) Personnel

Dr. D. categorizes the personnel requirement under the "No Brainer Category."

Unfortunately, I see way too many violations of the QSR, by device manufacturers, for

failing to establish requirements, including training of personnel working in controlled

environments. For starters, having personnel entering the controlled environment with

varying degrees of "toe jam" will quickly draw the attention of an FDA investigator

during one of their friendly visits. Now granted, no one appreciates wearing flip-flops

and cargo shorts more than Dr. D (except maybe Jimmy Buffett); however, this

California business casual look is not appropriate for controlled environments.

Additionally, some level of personal hygiene is expected. Furthermore, make-up

can be problematic, so if eyeliner and eyebrow liner are not permanently tattooed to the

face of the person entering the controlled environment (Michael Jackson style), or somehow capable of flaking off onto the work surfaces, it should not be worn. Moreover, open sores, cuts, etc. must be covered. In fact, employees that are in ill health should not be permitted to enter the controlled environment. Besides, why risk getting fellow employees sick. Finally, clothing that generates particulate, jewelry, and the wearing of hats, ball caps (especially LA Dodger caps – as Dr. D. is a Giants fan) needs to be included into the procedure for proper controlled environment etiquette. Remember, the regulation is very specific; *"each manufacturer shall establish and maintain requirements for the health, cleanliness, personal practices, and clothing of personnel if contact between such personnel and product or environment could reasonably be expected to have an adverse effect on product quality."*

(e) Contamination Control

Dr. D would like to tell you a brief story. Once upon a time, at a medical device manufacturer, in a faraway land known as California, the weekly surface contamination reports were placed upon the good doctor's desk. Typically, the weekly sampling of work surfaces with contact plates would yield 25-colony forming units (CFU) or less. In this particular report, the number was greater than 1,000 CFUs for one specific microorganism, with the notation of to many to count. When I asked the laboratory to perform a detailed assessment and identify the species, the investigation determined the offender was fecal matter. Are you kidding me? That being said, the moral of this story is to ensure all personnel entering the controlled environment are adequately trained in the ancient art form of hand washing, and not just with water.

It is now time for another Dr. D and his broken record time, "as with all aspects of production and process controls and the QSR, as a whole, **procedures are required**." In the case of contamination control, medical device manufacturer's need to prevent the induction of contamination into the manufacturing area. Additionally, device manufacturers need to test and monitor work surfaces, the surrounding air, and water for monthly bioburden and pyrogen levels.

So what does Dr. D. recommend as a baseline program for contamination control? It really does commence with good hygiene, appropriate operator clothing, gowning, hair covers, facial hair covers, sanitizing soap and water, finger cots, gloves, non-particulate generating clean room supplies, the frequent cleaning of work stations, a first-class janitorial service, etc. Of course, the approach to contamination control needs to be **placed into a well-written procedure**, and all personnel entering the controlled environment **must be trained to the procedure.** Just on a side note; when the agency does visit, ensure the FDA investigator is properly trained on gowning procedures, prior to allowing the investigator admittance into the controlled environment. Also, remember to document the training of the investigator. Additionally, ensure material moving into the clean room is free of particulate and enters through a restricted pass-through (positive pressure portal).

In the previous paragraphs, Dr. D. expanded on the prevention of contamination; however, monitoring for contamination is equally critical. Dr. D <u>does not</u> claim to be an expert on contamination other than to state; "germs are bad in the clean room." That being said, I came across an outstanding Internet site, while researching this book. The Microbiology Network contains multiple white papers pertaining to the topic of contamination control. It is a great site and well worth the visit. Dr. D recommends reviewing EN ISO 14644-1:1999, EN ISO 14644-2:2000, EN ISO 14644-3:2005, EN

ISO 14644-4:2001, EN ISO 14644-5:2004, EN ISO 14644-6:2007, EN ISO 14644-7:2004, and EN ISO 14644-8:2006. Collectively, these standards delineated the requirements for establishing, maintaining, and monitoring clean room environments. That being said, Dr. D. recommends the following monitoring steps be considered as part of sustaining effective contamination control.

1. Pyrogen and bioburden testing of waste water;

2. Pyrogen and bioburden testing on manufactured products (retains);

3. Establishing acceptable levels, alert limits, and action limits for contamination testing(aerobic bacterial and fungal) and particulate counts;

4. Monitoring particulate counts at randomly selected locations;

5. Random surface monitoring employing specially designed contact plates, e.g., Trypticase Soy Agar (TSA) or Sabouraud Dextros Agar (SDA); and

6. Random air sampling employing settling plates.

You will need to retain all of the records associated with environmental controls and contamination controls. Rest assured, the agency routinely reviews these records during their friendly visits, including the training records. Additionally, ensure all of the training records for personnel are current in regards to environmental controls and contamination controls. These records should include contractors entering the controlled environment. Finally, Dr. D. strongly recommends that environmental control and contamination control data be presented as part of management review.

As previously stated earlier in this chapter,, "The building requirement falls into Dr. D's category of not being rocket science." According to the QSR, *Buildings shall be of suitable design and contain sufficient space to perform necessary operations, prevent mix-ups, and assure orderly handling."* Simply put, the building and building layout for manufacturing medical devices requires some intelligent design. For example, you want to ensure material flows efficiently through the manufacturing cycle. Not wanting to over simplify the approach; (a) raw materials enter the building at one location, (b) inspected (as necessary), (c) placed into stores or Kan Ban, (d) kitted,(e) released to manufacturing, (f) assembled into finished medical devices, (g) submitted to final inspection, (h) cleaned, (i) packaged, (j) released for sterilization, and (k) shipped to the sterilizer at a location that is segregated from the material receipts location. For the most part, the flow is sequential and capable of preventing, as the QSR reflects, "mix-ups."

As part of the building requirement, device manufactures should also consider:

1. Sufficient space available to support manufacturing operations;

2. Defined area(s) for holding non-conforming product;

3. Defined holding areas for material pending receipt and evaluation

4. Clean and well-organized stockroom;

5. Plan for pest control;

6. Plan for disaster recovery (real important for areas prone to earth quakes, tornados, an hurricanes);

7. Adequate electrical drops available on the manufacturing floor;

8. Plumbing for compressed air, nitrogen, and other inert gases (as warranted);

9. Water (city or DI);

10. Office space;

11. Building maintenance;

12. Restrooms;

13. Lunch and break rooms; and

14. Parking.

Please keep in mind, Dr. D's list is not an all-inclusive one. My intent is to ensure device manufacturers take into consideration anything and everything in regards to the building that houses medical device manufacturing. Remember the old adage, "First impressions are lasting impressions."

Time for another Dr. Story – once upon a time, the doctor was asked to visit a supplier that specialized in wiring grinding. The for-cause visit was due to food particles (Cheetos® residue) being found on wires upon receipt. Seriously, would you like some Cheetos® with that guide wire? Now granted, wire grinding can result in extreme challenges for facility managers in the pursuit of maintaining a clean facility. However, I am sure the look of surprise on Dr. D's face, actually the look of shock on Dr. D's face was priceless, when the plant manager handed the good doctor a pair of guilloches, upon entering the building. **Are you kidding me?** What part of suitable environment was not understood by this supplier? The entire facility was covered in machine oil. Needless to say, Dr. D's visit was brief.

(g) Equipment

Let Dr. D repeat again – broken record time! Can you still say IQ, OQ, and PQ? If you cannot, you had better learn the meaning of installation qualification (IQ), operational qualification (OQ), and performance qualification (PQ). The regulation states; "*Each manufacturer shall ensure that all equipment used in the manufacturing process meets specified requirements and is appropriately designed, constructed, placed, and installed to facilitate maintenance, adjustment, cleaning, and use. "* What the agency is requiring from device manufacturers is documented in the following bullet points.

1. Ensure equipment and tooling, to be employed in the manufacture of medical device, is adequately documented. For example, if a piece of equipment is procured from an approved supplier, there should be a procurement specification. If equipment or tooling is manufactured internally, e.g., the model shop; the expectation is that a specification or drawing be created and given to the model shop for the project.

2. After it has been determined that equipment meets specification, the design of the equipment is robust, and the equipment has been installed, including the IQ, the real fun begins. The piece of equipment must be maintained and cleaned, adjustments and settings locked in, and the operators and maintenance technicians trained.

3. Additionally, operator and technician training, equipment operating instructions, maintenance, calibration, etc. shall be documented. Broken record time – DG Rule # 6 – All procedures, work instructions, drawings, specifications, etc. must be written, well-documented, and controlled within a defined document control system.

4. Furthermore, please do not forget the IQ, OQ, and PQ. The FDA has become extremely process focused; and they will ask to review documentation associated with these activities.

Maintenance Schedule

There is a plethora of calibration and maintenance software, such as Blue

Mountain, available for sale. Employment of software can really simplify the scheduling aspect of preventive and scheduled maintenance. All equipment will require some type of maintenance on a regular basis, daily, weekly, monthly, etc.; however, a subset of equipment will also require calibration and adjustments. Regardless, all activities associated with maintenance need to be documented. The documentation shall include a procedure defining the maintenance, cleaning, calibration, or adjustments being performed. Additionally, the records documenting the performance of these activities shall include the date, name, and signature of the person(s) performing the activities. Remember, DG Rule # 3 - Document the results of all events in writing, because if it is not documented in writing, the events did not occur.

Inspection

The regulation requires periodic inspections to ensure equipment is being maintained in accordance with the published maintenance schedule. In short, verifying the effectiveness of the entire maintenance program needs to be incorporated into the internal audit program. Depending upon how the inspection activities are employed on the manufacturing floor, tollgate versus audit inspection, random audits of processes, and the equipment employed for the processes is strongly recommended. Once again, remember to document all of the audit and random inspection activities, including the date, name, signature, and the results of each inspection.

Adjustments

Frankly, Dr. D hates adjustable equipment on the manufacturing floor, especially if the equipment requires frequent adjustments. Regardless, if adjustments to equipment need to be made, I suggest that these adjustments, tolerances, limitations, etc. be placed into a released procedure or template. Ensure the procedure or template is located at each station and the operators are reading and utilizing this documentation. Additionally, operators making these adjustments shall be trained and the training documented – broken record, the Doctor knows.

(h) Manufacturing Material

Broken record time! Once again, the need for procedures is clearly depicted in subsection h, which means DG Rule # 6 – All procedures, work instructions, drawings, specifications, etc. must be written, well-documented, and controlled within a defined document control system, continues to be a salient requirement. Besides, other than death and taxes, rest assured, the agency will expect to see written procedures that reflect ongoing compliance with the QSR. I hope that you readers have been able to glean the importance of procedures from Dr. D's ongoing insistence upon developing and adhering to well-written procedures. The doctor really is looking out for my reader's best interests.

When writing the procedure or procedures in support of the manufacturing material requirement, some of the areas that should be considered (not an all-inclusive list):

1. Identification and removal of manufacturing material that will have an adverse effect on device quality;

2. The quarantine and handling of material that has been identified as having an adverse effect on product quality;

3. Management of age-sensitive materials such as adhesives and epoxies;

4. Employment and disposal of chemicals as part of the manufacturing process;

5. Location of Material Safety Data Sheets (MSDS), as required;

6. Management of Kan Ban systems;

7. Material storage locations;

8. Material handling;

9. Material identification and traceability;

10. Line segregation and batch management practices to prevent the mix-up of manufacturing materials; and

11. The identification of ways to support the reduction of manufacturing material.

(i) Automated Processes

Let Dr. D begin by stating; "validation of all software is required and all changes to software must be validated, reviewed, and approved." Additionally, all activities associated with automated processes must be documented, in writing. Why? Broken-record time, "if the event or activity is not documented in writing, it simply did not happen." In fact, with no documented evidence, your organization will not be able to prove to the FDA that validation of software or changes to software occurred.

Focusing on the warning letters depicted in this chapter, the first thing to notice is the employment of computers to generate reports managing quality metrics and integral parts of the quality system, e.g., CAPA, need to be validated. Additionally, COTS needs to be validated before it is released for use in the manufacturing environment in support of performing quality functions, e.g., complaint management or customer returns. Furthermore, firmware, PALs, storage devices, etc. all need to have their uses validated. Finally, do not forget Dr. D's "black box" comment. If software, firmware, etc. drive the functionality (inputs and outputs), validation is required.

Takeaways from Chapter 10

The primary takeaways from this chapter are for the most part elementary.

1. The FDA demands that medical device manufacturers exhibit complete control over production and process controls. Procedures, documentation, execution, etc. are all salient requirements. The expectation is that verification/validation activities support all released product and processes (internal and external); and subsequent changes to product and processes.

2. External standards, applicable codes, workmanship standards, the employment of samples, etc., must also be considered, and their use validated; including manufacturing equipment (IQ, OQ, and PQ).

3. Written procedures and documented training are not only mandatory, but provide for your best defense when the agency decides to bless your organization with one of their friendly visits.

4. Remember sustaining a controlled environment, providing appropriate training for employees and contractors entering the controlled environment, and keeping contamination from encroaching upon the controlled environment – specifically the medical devices being manufactured, is the proverbial low hanging fruit. Yes, it does take time and money to develop a fully functional and compliant controlled environment. However, in the medical device industry the cost of compliance is in reality the price of admission.

5. Invest in and design a world-class manufacturing facility.

6. Invest in equipment capable of supporting device manufacturing.

7.   Manufacturing material can be tailored to a device manufacturer's environment.

8.   The validation of all software employed by device manufacturers is required.

9.   In regards to the manufacturing environment, it is important to ensure that other procedures documenting compliance to related QSR requirements, similar to non-conforming product, be aligned with the manufacturing materials procedure(s).

10.   For automated processes, do not fall into the COTS trap by assuming the software has been validated by the developer; and is suitable for use in the medical device industry. When in doubt, Dr. D recommends asking for a copy of the validation report from the developer. Even if the developer has validated the software, your still need to ensure that the software and the validation is appropriate for your application.

In closing, remember - when the agency comes to visit your facility, and trust Dr. D when he states, "eventually an investigator will end up on your doorsteps," the initial impressions made will be lasting impressions. Equipment maintenance, IQ, OQ, PQ, calibration, operator training, technician training, written procedures, records, etc. are basic requirements for compliance with section 820.70 of the QSR. Written records of these activities are always your best defense, when sitting across from the FDA investigator, during one of their friendly visits. Finally, always remember FDA visits are formal investigations (collecting evidence) versus audits performed by notified bodies.

Chapter 11 – Inspection, Measuring, and Test Equipment

21 CFR, Part 820

Subpart G

Section 820.72

Chapter 11 – Inspection, Measuring, and Test Equipment

In Chapter 11, the doctor continues with his on-going prolegomenon (look-it-up if you need to) examination of the Quality System Regulations (QSR) while continuing to provide insight and guidance for compliance. Inspection, measuring, and test equipment, in the opinion of Dr. D, forms a significant part of the quality-system foundation for successful medical device manufacturers. At the end of the day, device manufactures need effective tools to gage adherence to approved product specifications; and the vehicle employed for doing so, is the performance of acceptance activities utilizing inspection, measuring, and test equipment.

Warning Letter Violation

Being an old quality guy (yes - Dr. D is a little long in the proverbial tooth), nothing raises the doctor's hackles more than compliance issues associated with calibration or should I say lack of calibration. This chapter's warning-letter extraction depicts procedural issues, execution issues, the utilization of equipment with expired calibration, equipment with documented functional performance issues, and to top it off, these are repeat violations from this device manufacturer's previous inspection. **Hello! What are you thinking?** Calibration is the foundation for acceptance activities and the effective employment of inspection, measuring, and test equipment. **Hello!** Every single investigator, auditor, internal auditor; customer auditor, and hopefully; mechanical inspector understands the significance of calibration and the employment of calibrated equipment as part of acceptance activities. In regards to the warning letter in support of this chapter, the management team leading this device manufacturer should not only be embarrassed, they should be ashamed. In fact, please consider this an official **"shame on you"** from Dr. D. I only hope Deming is not rolling over in his final resting place. I am sorry but Dr. D is not finished venting, "Using equipment that has not been calibrated – hello – what are you thinking?" It is the doctor's strong opinion; "Perfidious (look-up time) violators of the QSR are well-deserving of the enforcement actions taken by the FDA."

In an earlier chapter of this book, I introduced the concept of the orange jumpsuit, typically associated with convicted felons. In support of this chapter, Dr. D would like to reintroduce the acronym, (CJO) or Chief Jailable Officer. In linking the two, the CJO can be on the receiving end of this orange jumpsuit, if found criminally liable as part of enforcement actions pursued by the agency.

Just in case you are wondering, some friends of Dr. D, asked the doctor if he would look good in the proverbial orange jumpsuit? Dr. D politely responded; "the jumpsuit would need to be green to reflect my Irish roots." Maybe a compromise is in order, an orange jumpsuit with green stripes.

Warning Letter (May 2010)

> **Observation 7 of 12**. *Failure to establish and maintain adequate procedures to ensure that equipment is routinely calibrated, inspected, checked, and maintained to include provisions for handling, preservation, and storage of equipment, so that its accuracy and fitness for use are maintained, as required by 21 CFR 820.72(a). This is a repeat observation from FDA 483 issued on 11/20/07. For example:*
>
> > *a. The Lyophilizer Maintenance and Calibration Procedure (Q56-P14, Revision 02) specified that lyophilizers are to undergo quarterly preventative maintenance by a licensed contractor. However, quarterly preventive maintenance has not been executed for the VirTis and Hull Lyophilizers. Additionally, the firm admitted that quarterly maintenance procedures have not been performed by a licensed contractor.*
>
> > *b. A product technician at the firm admitted that the chart recorder used on the VirTis Lyophilizer to document lyophilization parameters has not been functioning*

since mid December 2009. No service work order had been initiated to repair the broken recorder.

c. The digital caliper (Equipment ill # (b)(4) used in receiving inspection activities is overdue for annual calibration. Last calibration was performed in 10/30/08.

FDA Response to Observation 7 of 12. *We have reviewed your response and concluded that it is not adequate. You stated that you completed a review of your maintenance schedule and reminders have been entered into Outlook. However, you did not state if the lyophilizers and calipers would be immediately calibrated. Also, you stated that the VirTis operator was retrained but did not provide documentation of the training.*

Quality System Regulation - 21 CFR, Part 820

QSR – Subpart G – Production and Process Controls

Section 820.72 Inspection, Measuring, and Test Equipment

(a)Control of inspection, measuring, and test equipment. Each manufacturer shall ensure that all inspection, measuring, and test equipment, including mechanical, automated, or electronic inspection and test equipment, is suitable for its intended purposes and is capable of producing valid results. Each manufacturer shall establish and maintain procedures to ensure that equipment is routinely calibrated, inspected, checked, and maintained. The procedures shall include provisions for handling, preservation, and storage of equipment, so that its accuracy and fitness for use are maintained. These activities shall be documented.

(b)Calibration. Calibration procedures shall include specific directions and limits for accuracy and precision. When accuracy and precision limits are not met, there shall be provisions for remedial action to reestablish the limits and to evaluate whether there was any adverse effect on the device's quality. These activities shall be documented.

(1)Calibration standards. Calibration standards used for inspection, measuring, and test equipment shall be traceable to national or international standards. If national or international standards are not practical or available, the manufacturer shall use an independent reproducible standard. If no applicable standard exists, the manufacturer shall establish and maintain an in-house standard.

(2)Calibration records. The equipment identification, calibration dates, the individual performing each calibration, and the next calibration date shall be documented. These records shall be displayed on or near each piece of equipment or shall be readily available to the personnel using such equipment and to the individuals responsible for calibrating the equipment.

Inspection, Measuring and Test Equipment

I must admit, the doctor struggles to fathom the logic behind device

manufacturers not having robust procedures and processes in support of inspection, measuring, and test equipment. Failure to comply with this requirement, in the opinion of Dr. D, is the equivalent to what I will call a "compliance mortal sin." Process control, acceptance activities, engineering studies, validations (IQ, OQ, PQ), product design and development, and even more important, ensuring finished medical devices are safe and effective, are premised on the application of effective inspection, measurement, and test equipment practices. Remember, the entire approach to inspection, measuring, and test equipment fails when calibration practices are inadequate or completely ignored. Yes, the doctor understands that calibration is an expensive and time-consuming investment. However, broken-record time, the costs associated with calibration activities can be unequivocally categorized as mandatory and considered part of the price for admission into the medical device industry.

Dr. D Story Time – Once upon a time, in a land called the United States, Dr. D was visiting a new supplier candidate. On this particular business trip, the good doctor had been in an automobile accident on the morning of the scheduled audit. Dr. D unceremoniously ended the life of one of Bambi's relatives on Interstate 80 in Pennsylvania. For some reason, Bambi's cousin felt compelled to attack Dr. D's car, while he was driving 65 miles-per-hour on the Interstate. Needless to say, the deer lost this battle but inflicted some serious pain on the doctor. Eventually, Dr. D made it to the doorstep of this supplier, a day later than expected, and extremely sore from the accident (airbags leave nasty marks, bruises, and an occasionally broken rib or two). My sense of humor, which I needed desperately for this visit, was void, lost in the pain, and grimacing. During the initial walk through, besides not having a recognizable quality system, Dr. D observed that most of the inspection, measuring, and test equipment, employed by this potential supplier, had expired calibration but was still in use. The calibration stickers depicted over-due calibration dates approaching two-years. My scheduled two-day visit was over before lunchtime, on the first day. Can you say – not approved? My parting gift to this potential supplier was the awarding of just one deviation. Yes, Dr. D felt like being generous. As I recall the deviation was worded; "no identifiable or cohesive quality system exists. Please provide a detailed plan, delineating a path toward establishing a quality system that is in compliance with EN ISO 13485."

Story Epilogue - A year later, the supplier contacted Dr. D and asked if they were still being considered for the project. I was compelled to ask if the installment of a recognizable quality system had occurred. The answer absolutely floored the doctor; "No, we are waiting for the purchase order before we start." I politely responded, "Have a nice day" and then there was a click, as Dr. D hung up the telephone – end of story.

Control of Inspection, Measuring and Test Equipment

So what is the agency looking for in regards to control? For starters, rocket science time again, the expectation is that inspection, measuring, and test equipment, employed as part of the device manufacturing process, is suitable for its intended use. The results obtained, from the employment of test equipment, must be capable of producing repeatable, reproducible, and valid results. It is the opinion of Dr. D, the only way to achieve repeatable, reproducible, and valid results is through the application of verification and validation activities for all inspection, measuring, and test equipment. A Dr. D watch out - be very careful about claiming the results obtained are self-evident, because other than death or taxes, very few things in the medical device industry fall into the category of self-evident; and if they do, a written rationale will be required to justify the self-evident claim. Additionally, the expectation is that some resemblance of a maintenance and calibration system exists, with the system documented by written procedure(s). No surprise, right? Furthermore, the handling, preservation, and storage of equipment is not only important, it needs to be captured in a procedure. For example, if your organization is storing microscopes, oscilloscopes, or similar pieces of equipment in the janitor's closet, alongside the mops, mop-buckets, and the brooms; the FDA will probably take exception to the practice. In reality, the investigator will issue the infamous Form 483; and you can take that to the bank. Finally, all activities associated with this requirement shall be documented. Why? Because the QSR clearly states the documented activities requirement; and documented evidence is always your best defense during a friendly visit, by the agency.

Calibration

Since you already know how strongly the doctor feels about the importance of calibration, I will cut right to the chase. As with all requirements associated with the QSR, strict adherence to DG Rule # 6 – "All procedures, work instructions, drawings, specifications, etc. must be written, well-documented, and controlled with in a defined document control system" is mandatory. In fact, the procedures for calibration need to be prescriptive in regards to determining and verifying limits for accuracy and precision.

Additionally, if during the execution of routine calibration it is determined that a piece of equipment is no longer within published operating specifications, remedial action shall be pursued. So what does that mean Dr. D? In short, at least two actions will need to be pursued. (1) The piece of equipment must be repaired, calibrated, adjusted, etc., to ensure it is once again operating within established parameters or the manufacturer's specification. If equipment cannot be repaired, it needs to be identified, tagged, and removed from service. It is a bad practice to leave out-of-tolerance or broken inspection, measuring, and test equipment on the manufacturing floor, without some type of label or tag (preferably red), informing the entire world that, "this piece of equipment shall not be used." The best practice is to remove the piece of equipment; whenever possible, from the manufacturing floor. (2) Formal corrective action needs to be pursued to ensure devices manufactured during the time-period between when the last documented calibration was performed and when the out-of-specification condition occurred, are still acceptable for use (a.k.a., safe and effective for their intended use).

Furthermore, if the quality influence on finished medical devices, resulting from an out-of-tolerance condition relating to inspection, measuring, or test equipment cannot be determined; be prepared for that ugly six-letter word, **RECALL!** That is why batch control is so important. Effective batch management can limit the exposure due to operating anomalies such as calibration and equipment non-conformances.

Finally, yes - all activities associated with this requirement "broken-record time" shall be documented. Why – because documented evidence is always your best defense during a friendly visit from the agency. I hope Dr. D's many mantras are beginning to sink in.

Calibration Standards

Since the FDA governs device manufacturers building finished devices for introduction into commerce within the Unites States and its protectorates, the expectation is that the calibration system shall be premised on a national standard. In the United States, that standard is the National Institute for Standards and Technology (NIST). Now

Dr. D is going to head out onto that proverbial tree limb and assume that most device manufacturers maintain primary and/or transfer standards that are NIST traceable. Dr. D will also assume that most medical device manufacturers retain a metrology service to perform calibration on standards, and potentially on all inspection, measuring, and test equipment employed during the manufacturing process. If your organization is creating standards because no external standard exists, these standards need to be validated. The output of the standard must be repeatable, reproducible, and provide valid results.

Calibration Records

Although record retention is important for all aspects of the QSR, calibration records should probably be elevated to a mission-critical status. Traceability, back to a national standard, for specific pieces of inspection, measuring, and test equipment is mandatory. Additionally, the calibration records, for each piece of inspection, measuring, and test equipment should reflect, as a minimum:

1. The date calibration was performed;

2. The name of the technician performing the calibration;

3. The next calibration due date;

4. A list of primary and secondary standards, including their calibration status, employed as part of the calibration;

5. A printout / recording of adjustments made;

6. A printout / recording of key operational characteristics verified;

7. A notation of performance limitations; and

8. A detailed analysis of out-of-tolerance conditions, including corrections.

   Furthermore, all pieces of inspection, measuring, and test equipment shall be clearly identified with a unique serial number and a calibration sticker or label that reflects; (a) date calibrated, (b) name of technician performing the calibration, and (c) the date calibration is due. Make sure inspectors and operators are properly trained, so they never use equipment reflecting an expired calibration status.

Finally, although the QSR is not overly prescriptive in regards to what should be retained in the calibration files or what a procedure should reflect. However, EN ISO 17025 is very prescriptive in regards to good calibration laboratory practices. Dr. D strongly recommends that medical device manufacturers should refrain from employing metrology facilities and other outside testing laboratories that are not EN ISO 17025 compliant. Employing metrology labs that are certified to EN ISO 17025 is really the best practice to pursue.

Other Procedural Considerations for Calibration

Now granted, the depth and detail required for supporting compliance with the inspection, measuring, and test equipment will vary depending on organizational structure, size, need, etc. Some of the bulleted items depicted below deserve consideration when drafting procedures to support calibration:

1. A policy for the introduction of new inspection, measuring and test equipment into use;

2. A policy for the removal of equipment;

3. A policy for lost equipment;

4. A policy for equipment storage;

5. An all-inclusive list of equipment, including the calibration status and location (aka, calibration-recall list};

6. A policy for addressing out-of-tolerance events;

7. A policy for expired / past-due calibration;

8. Calibration intervals;

9. Calibration ranges and accuracies;

10. Storage of primary and secondary standards;

11. The calibration, identification, and employment of equipment owned by employees (note: common in machine shops; however, Dr. D believes this is a bad practice);

12. The assessment of metrology and other external labs (extremely important);

13. A definition and list of the records retained in the individual equipment files;

14. Inclusion of the calibration system into the internal audit function;

15. Individual procedures for each piece of equipment calibrated internally;

16. Employment of tamper-proof seals, when warranted;

17. Different classes of calibration, e.g., calibration required versus no-calibration required;

18. Equipment traceability;

19. Environmental conditions; and

20. Training (extremely important).

Once again, Dr. D does not claim that this list is all-inclusive. However, if device manufacturers can wordsmith these bullet points into a procedure or series of procedures, the outcome will probably be viewed as favorable during an FDA visit; providing the procedures are being followed.

Takeaways from Chapter 11

In wrapping up Chapter 11, the first takeaway is the employment of an effective approach to calibration control, including procedures to support the inspection, measuring, and test equipment requirement delineated within the QSR. The second takeaway is that calibration is one of the key building blocks supporting the foundation for an effective quality system. The third takeaway is that the accuracy of acceptance activities is premised on calibration and the accuracy of the inspection, measuring, and test equipment employed. The fourth takeaway is that non-conformances associated with inspection, measuring, and test equipment can result in product recalls. The fifth and final takeaway, as always, documented evidence is your best defense during a friendly visit from the FDA.

Chapter 12 – Process Validation

21 CFR, Part 820

Subpart G

Section 820.75

Chapter 12 – Process Validation

In this chapter, the doctor provides his guidance for 21 CFR, Part 820 – Subpart G (Production and Process Controls) with a review of, and guidance for, compliance with section 820.75, Process Validation (PV). Medical device manufacturers must ensure all processes are either verified or validated. The first of two salient points to remember are that processes that cannot be verified through the employment of inspection or testing shall be validated; henceforth, the name process validation. Pretty simple, right? The second salient point is that process verification is simply the verification that process outputs meet requirements delineated through the market and product specifications (a.k.a., inputs). In short, the assembly line must employ processes capable of manufacturing devices that meet their requirements, including intended use, while ensuring device safety and efficacy are sustained. As discussed in previous chapters in this book, the key components of process validation are: (a) Installation Qualification (IQ); (b) Operational Qualification (OQ); and (c) Performance Qualification (PQ). One final comment, Dr. D strongly recommends a visit to the Global Harmonization Task Force (GHTF) website. Visitors can download the guidance provided for PV. The link for the GHTF website is depicted under the reference section at the end of this book.

Warning Letter Violation

PV continues to be an increasing and pressing concern for the agency; and this concern is reflected in an increase in enforcement actions pursued. There has been a significant increase in the issuance of warning letters depicting PV compliance violations. These violations are premised on Form 483 observations noted during the friendly visits by the FDA, formally and appropriately named "*inspections*." The warning-letter extraction, in support of this chapter, depicts a device manufacturer that has failed to adequately validate a process that could not be verified by subsequent test or inspection; with a high degree of accuracy, I might add. On the positive side, the warning letter recipient had an established procedure for performing process validation. Unfortunately, they deviated from their established procedure. In an effort to further irritate the FDA, the initial response to this observation was deemed unacceptable. Why? The formal investigation, as part of the CAPA process, was not complete.

Dr. D is quite serious in stating; "the Barmecidal (look-it up if you must) amount of warning letters being issued by the FDA, is not just a facade, they really exist in significant volume." As I have recommended frequently, throughout this book, Dr. D strongly recommends a visit to the fda.gov website, and spending some time traversing the enforcement action page, specifically, warning letters. Remember, warning letters do not just appear out of thin air. They are a direct result of the issuance of Form 483(s), premised on observations noted, during FDA investigations. Trust Dr. D when I say, "A warning letter opens an entirely new world of hurt and pain for organizations on the receiving end of this enforcement action."

Warning Letter (July 2010)

Observation 1 of 4 - *Failure to adequately validate with a high degree of assurance and approve according to established procedures, a process that cannot be fully verified by subsequent inspection and test as required by 21 CFR 820.75(a). For example, section (b)(4) of Document (b)(4), (b)(4), requires a (b)(4) sample for quality control testing and inspection. Section (b)(4) of this document describes (b)(4) for each of the (b)(4) on the (b)(4). For lot #s 0804427, 0804521 and 0804624 the (b)(4) sample for quality control testing and inspection was not performed as required by section (b)(4). For lot #s 0811405 and 0811433 the (b)(4) were not performed as required by section (b)(4).*

FDA's Response to Observation 1 of 4 - *We have reviewed your response dated*

March 26, 2010, and have concluded that its adequacy cannot be determined at this time. You have initiated and CAPA investigation to determine the failure to follow the protocol and have acknowledged that the failure did occur. However, you have not completed the investigation and have not provided documentation of the investigation or the corrective action.

Quality System Regulation - 21 CFR, Part 820

QSR – Subpart G – Production and Process Controls

Section 820.75 Process Validation

> *a) Where the results of a process cannot be fully verified by subsequent inspection and test, the process shall be validated with a high degree of assurance and approved according to established procedures. The validation activities and results, including the date and signature of the individual(s) approving the validation and where appropriate the major equipment validated, shall be documented.*

> *(b) Each manufacturer shall establish and maintain procedures for monitoring and control of process parameters for validated processes to ensure that the specified requirements continue to be met.*

> > *(1) Each manufacturer shall ensure that validated processes are performed by qualified individual(s).*

> > *(2) For validated processes, the monitoring and control methods and data, the date performed, and, where appropriate, the individual(s) performing the process or the major equipment used shall be documented.*

> > *(c) When changes or process deviations occur, the manufacturer shall review and evaluate the process and perform revalidation where appropriate. These activities shall be documented.*

Process Validation

The Doctor cannot fathom device manufacturers not having robust procedures and processes in support of PV. In fact, Dr. D has worked for an organization that has been on the receiving end of the agency's wrath because of a less-than stellar approach to validating processes. According to the GHTF guidance on PV (page 3), "In general, the validation of a process is the mechanism or system used by the manufacturer to plan, obtain data, record data, and interpret data." Additionally, the GHTF approach to process validation reinforces the generally accepted practice of employing IQ, OQ, and PQ as part of a robust approach to PV.

Procedures

Broken-record time again by Dr. D – written procedures, a.k.a. DG Rule # 6 – All procedures, work instructions, drawings, specifications, etc. must be written, well-documented, and controlled within a defined document control system, are mandatory in support of QSR requirements. Once again, deferring to the GHTF guidance, there are multiple inputs into establishing a world-class approach for PV. For starters, organizations really need to understand what processes require validation versus processes requiring verification only. For example, in the medical device industry, specifically sterile products, the approach to sterilization must be validated, EO, Gamma, steam, etc. The visual inspection of a catheter handle, to ascertain correct color, e.g., green versus white, will probably require a simple verification. Regardless, the approach chosen by device manufacturers must be <u>documented and defendable</u>, when sitting across from the FDA, during one of their friendly visits.

So what requirements need to be considered when developing an approach to PV and the subsequent delineation of the approach within a written procedure or procedures? Recommendations from the GHTF and additional recommendations from Dr. D, deserving of consideration for inclusion into written procedures and protocols, are:

1. Identifying organizational members for inclusion on the validation team;
2. Decision to pursue validation versus verification (recommend using the GHTF flow chart – page 6);
3. Definition of process inputs, outputs, data, and outcomes;
4. Creation of Master Validation Plan (MVP);

5. Generation of validation protocols;

6. Selection of tools, measuring, inspection, and test equipment;

7. Ensuring employed test methods, measuring, inspection, and test equipment is validated and calibrated;

8. Define organizational requirements for IQ, OQ, and PQ (i.e., what, how, how many, and when to verify or measure);

9. Sample size requirements;

10. Identify statistical techniques to be employed for data analysis and normality testing, i.e., Anderson-Darling; ANOVA, Ppk, etc.

11. Challenge versus limit testing;

12. Define the content, including review and approval requirements for Master Validation Reports (MVR);

13. Ensure pass and fail criteria is clearly defined in procedures and protocols;

14. Define documentation, retention, and storage of Protocols and MVRs (e.g., DHF);

15. Define requirements for ongoing monitoring and control of processes;

16. Establish requirements for when revalidation is required (e.g. relocating a production line);

17. Define when the employment of historical data is acceptable; and

18. Define the requirement for Gauge Repeatability and Reproducibility (R & R) Studies.

Performance of Validated Processes

As depicted in the list above (number 1), the personnel responsible for providing

121

input into the protocols, writing the protocols, reviewing and approving the protocols, and reviewing and approving the reports, need to be identified. The requirement is very specific in that Section 820.75 (1) requires validations to be executed by qualified individuals. Additionally, these qualified individuals will need to be trained to the released PV procedures employed by the device manufacturer. Furthermore, qualified individuals executing the protocols (operators, technicians, and engineers) also need to be trained. The training should encompass execution of protocols, data collection, data analysis, etc. Finally, all test anomalies identified during protocol execution require evaluation. The analysis must be to root-cause, with all actions, corrective, preventive, or otherwise; documented and retained. Dr. D strongly recommends installing a section for addressing deviations into the MVR, including pointers to requests for corrective and preventive action (CAPA) and relevant non-conformance reports (NCR's).

Monitoring and Control of Validated Processes

From a monitoring perspective, the QSR requires that the methods employed for the testing and subsequent collection of data must be controlled, including the validation of all test methods employed. As part of the control methods employed, the date executed, the name and signature of the person or persons performing the testing, a list of the equipment used, and all relevant data associated with protocol execution should be captured and retained. Remember, the execution and results of the validated processes "shall be documented." Why? Because according to DG Rule # 3 - Document the results of all events in writing, because if it is not documented in writing, the event did not occur. Broken record time – remember documented evidence is always your best defense, when sitting across from an FDA Investigator. As Deming would say; "In God we trust, all others bring data."

Process Changes and Deviations

Dr. D would like to share a little industry insight that is extremely important to the FDA. If changes to a process are made or deviations to a process noted, device manufacturers shall perform revalidation activities, where appropriate. Additionally, depending upon the device classification, you will need to notify the agency. Can you say 30-day PMA Supplement? Regardless, all changes need to be assessed and a path of revalidation considered, where appropriate. Finally, all activities associated with process changes, deviations, and associated revalidation activities shall be documented.

Takeaways from Chapter 12

The key takeaways from this chapter are: (a) download and read GHTF/SG3/N99-10:2004; (b) employ the GHTF as a guide for creating a robust procedure for process validation; (c) clearly define when validation will be pursued versus verification; (d) ensure all personnel associated with the process validation process are trained (including operators, technicians, and engineers; (e) evaluate all process changes and deviations and revalidate as appropriate; and (f) document the results. Treat process validation as a mission-critical activity. Your manufacturing folks will appreciate receiving processes that are fully validated and robust, as will the physicians using these devices to treat their patients.

Chapter 13 – Acceptance Activities

21 CFR, Part 820

Subpart H

Sections 820.80 & 820.86

Chapter 13 – Acceptance Activities

In this chapter, the doctor provides guidance for 21 CFR, Part 820 – Subpart – H, Acceptance Activities, and specifically (820.80), receiving, in-process, and finished device acceptance. Acceptance activities, especially receiving inspection (RI), are near and dear to Dr. D's heart, and yes, the doctor does have a heart. In pursuit of my doctorate, I spent the better part of two years collecting and analyzing data associated with the execution of RI. The data and subsequent analysis, depicted within my doctoral dissertation (Exploring the Effectiveness of Defensive-Receiving Inspection for Medical Device Manufacturers: a Mixed-Method Study), pointed to one conclusion. There is only limited value in performing old-school RI. However, there is substantial value in developing your strategic-supplier base by providing these suppliers with the tools needed to develop robust processes. The goal is to collaborate with suppliers capable of manufacturing products that meet your specifications. Additionally, these suppliers are capable of providing meaningful inspection and statistical data that can be employed in support of reducing the burden of RI. The end-result is RI resources can quickly analyze the data provided with, or shipped ahead of, received product. The reduction in inspection burden allows these valuable resources to be allocated to other activities such as First-Article-Inspection (FAI) in support of product development. Finally, there are fiscal savings associated with reducing the RI burden, with the most notable being the reduction in the number of inspectors required to support the RI function.

Warning Letter Violation

For this chapter, Dr. D has extracted violations from recently awarded warning letters. I think award is the appropriate vernacular, in this example, as the agency is legally able to award warning letters for bad, or should I say, non-compliant behavior. In general, the FDA frequently cites violators of section 820.80. The recipients of this these warning-letter extractions have violated two of the doctor's cardinal rules; (a) DG Rule # 6 (having written procedures), and (b) DG Rule #3 (documenting the results). Trust Dr. D. when I say, "not having robust procedures or documented results, in support of acceptance activities, will result in an intense colloquy (look-up-time) between management and the FDA, prior to the investigator issuing the user-friendly Form 483."

Another Dr. D watch out is the correct way to respond to a Form 483 observation or warning letter. An offending device manufacturer cannot simply reply by stating; "the problem has been fixed or a procedure has been generated." Why? Although supposedly there are no dumb questions, this particular "why" question should be categorized as dumb. A Form 483 or warning letter, when issued, are the precursory steps taken in pursuit of additional enforcement action pursued by the agency. The FDA requires **OBJECTIVE EVIDENCE** to support the closure of observations noted within the Form 483 or warning letter. Repeat after me, "objective evidence" good.

Warning Letter One (June 2010)

Observation 3 of 6 – *Failure to establish and maintain procedures for acceptance of incoming product as required by 21 CFR § 820.80(b). Specifically, your firm has failed to establish a written procedure for incoming product to be inspected, tested, or otherwise verified as conforming to specified requirements. This was a repeat violation from a previous inspection.*

Warning Letter Two (May 2010)

Observation 4 of 12 - *Failure to adequately document acceptance activities to include the results, as required by 21 CFR 820.80(e)(3). For example:*

a. Packaging Specification Sheets for a Foil Pouch (POU-055 - D03-ES123 - Revision 03) and the Raw Material Specification Sheet for Temperature Indicator (TEM-001 -

D03-DS182 - Revision 04) listed the acceptable dimensions and functional testing requirements, however, the receiving inspection records did not include the measurements taken or the results of the functional testing performed on these materials by the QC inspector.

b. Raw Material Specification Sheet for a Urine Cup (UCP-009 - D03-DS78 - Revision 02) listed acceptable dimensions for the cup, but the receiving inspection records did not include the measurements taken to demonstrate that the incoming cup met the documented raw material specifications.

*c. Specialty Chemical Specification Sheet for a Methadone BSAJBTG Antigen Conjugate (9MAD-01 - D03-BS074 - Revision 02)) required that the material had a minimum purity of **(b)(4)** but the raw material inspection records did not contain any evidence that this purity was met.*

FDA's Response to Observation 4 of 12 - *We have reviewed your response and concluded that it is not adequate because you did not provide any documentation of the corrective action. You stated that specifications on raw materials needed to be reviewed and updated to reflect actual testing performed and new documents will be created to record the results. You stated that the process, and presumably, the documents will be completed by 2/28/10.*

Observation 5 of 12 - *Failure to establish and maintain procedures for acceptance of incoming product. Incoming product shall be inspected, tested, or otherwise verified as conforming to specified requirements. Acceptance or rejection shall be documented, as required by 21 CFR 820.80(b). For example, you do not have a procedure in place to test the purity of Methadone BSAJBTG Antigen Conjugate and the specification sheet provided by the vendor does not specify the purity level of the material.*

FDA's Response to Observation 5 of 12 - *We have reviewed your response and concluded that is not adequate because you did not provide a procedure for testing the purity of the Methadone BSA/BTG Antigen Conjugate.*

Quality System Regulation - 21 CFR, Part 820

QSR – Subpart H – Acceptance Activities

Section 820.80 Receiving, In-process, and Finished Device Acceptance

(a)General. Each manufacturer shall establish and maintain procedures for acceptance activities. Acceptance activities include inspections, tests, or other verification activities.

(b)Receiving acceptance activities. Each manufacturer shall establish and maintain procedures for acceptance of incoming product. Incoming product shall be inspected, tested, or otherwise verified as conforming to specified requirements. Acceptance or rejection shall be documented.

(c)In-process acceptance activities. Each manufacturer shall establish and maintain acceptance procedures, where appropriate, to ensure that specified requirements for in-process product are met. Such procedures shall ensure that in-process product is

controlled until the required inspection and tests or other verification activities have been completed, or necessary approvals are received, and are documented.

(d)Final acceptance activities. Each manufacturer shall establish and maintain procedures for finished device acceptance to ensure that each production run, lot, or batch of finished devices meets acceptance criteria. Finished devices shall be held in quarantine or otherwise adequately controlled until released. Finished devices shall not be released for distribution until:
    (1) The activities required in the DMR are completed;
    (2) the associated data and documentation is reviewed;
    (3) the release is authorized by the signature of a designated individual(s); and
    (4) the authorization is dated.

(e)Acceptance records. Each manufacturer shall document acceptance activities required by this part. These records shall include:
    (1) The acceptance activities performed;
    (2) the dates acceptance activities are performed;
    (3) the results;
    (4) the signature of the individual(s) conducting the acceptance activities; and
    (5) where appropriate the equipment used. These records shall be part of the DHR.

Section 820.86 Acceptance Status

Each manufacturer shall identify by suitable means the acceptance status of product, to indicate the conformance or nonconformance of product with acceptance criteria. The identification of acceptance status shall be maintained throughout manufacturing, packaging, labeling, installation, and servicing of the product to ensure that only product which has passed the required acceptance activities is distributed, used, or installed.

General

The general requirement is a Dr. D no-brainer. Device manufacturers are required to write, maintain, train to, and comply with their procedures in support of all acceptance activities. Additionally, these acceptance activities should include physical inspection, testing, verification, data collection, analysis, and all other activities that can be remotely construed as acceptance. My recommendation is to invest some time, effort and of course money into establishing your organization's approach to performing acceptance activities. Effective acceptance activities can be your first-line of defense against the introduction of defects into finished medical devices, while reducing the potential for expensive market withdraws, a.k.a., RECALLS. Yes, RECALLS are ugly; unfortunately, they continue to be a reality in the medical device industry.

Receiving Acceptance Activities

In the introduction for this chapter, Dr. D expanded on his opinion of receiving acceptance activities. In short, I find little value in the antiquated approaches many device manufacturers employ in support of RI. Remember, the fundamental requirement, as stated within the QSR is, "Incoming product shall be inspected, tested, or otherwise verified as conforming to specified requirements." It does not state you must perform 100% visual or mechanical inspection on every-single product procured and received. That is why Dr. D supports a well-documented approach to reduced inspection activities, especially at RI. I am a big proponent of establishing a fundamentally sound and statistically-based approach to inspection, executed by the supplier, and verified by the procuring activity, in support of reducing the overall inspection burden.

Through the employment of an interactive approach to supplier management, with active supplier participation, using tools such as the collection and analysis of measurement data can result in a reduction in the amount of receiving acceptance activities pursued. In conjunction with the FAI process, it is a reasonable expectation that the specification creators glom the opportunity and work with the suppliers in the determination of critical features requiring monitoring and measurement data, in support of a Supplier Statistical Data Program (SSDP). Your suppliers should have the capability to identify the critical features and dimensions needed to gage the overall effectiveness of their manufacturing processes, and the sustainability of long-term process control. For an effective SSDP to work, there must by a collaborative approach pursued, between the supplier and manufacturer, for identifying the features and characteristics requiring inspection and measurement. Additionally, the determination of whether the data collected should contain attribute data or variable data; and targeted process capability indices (Ppk) occurs as part of the development process. Can you say Ppk of 2.0 (Six Sigma)? Furthermore, risk indices needs to be considered for all components placed into the program when establishing a SSDP. The FMEA, and I hope you are using them, should assist in determining the appropriate levels of risk. Finally, once agreement is reached on what should be included within the SSD Agreement (SSDA); the agreement should be reviewed, approved, and signed by both parties (supplier and device manufacturer). One final thought, after launching a SSDP, you will need to keep your suppliers honest. What does that mean Dr. D? It means you will need to occasionally inspect lots received as part of the SSDP and verify your measurement results match that of your suppliers. Regardless of the tools employed as part of complying with the receiving acceptance requirement, all of the results shall be documented and retained. Why? By now, you should know this answer; having documented results equates to supporting evidence, which is always your best defense during a friendly visit by the FDA.

In-Process Acceptance Activities

Not unlike receiving acceptance activities, device manufacturers spend a significant amount of time and money in pursuit of in-process acceptance activities. Once again, the regulation does not state, "thou shall 100% inspect and test every-single device as part of the normal manufacturing flow." What device manufacturers need to do is establish robust and validated processes, well-written manufacturing and inspection instructions, and pursue in-process inspection activities, that are premised on a documented statistical approach. Remember the agency is big on employing validation and verification.

For example, electrophysiological catheters are complex Class 3 devices (US) that contain a significant amount of wiring and electrical connections. A 100% in-process electrical test may be warranted due to device complexity. However, catheter-working length, with a wide tolerance may require only a sample inspection, maybe an AQL of 4.0. Regardless, each device manufacturer gets to establish an _effective_ approach for pursuing in-process acceptance activities. I underlined effective, in the previous sentence, because regardless of the approach pursued, it will need to be defendable as effective to the FDA. For example, if the yields for catheter-working length are low, then justifying an AQL of 4.0 is going to be difficult to defend. Besides, effective in-process acceptance activities not only place the business at risk (Recalls), they can quickly erode margins due to excessive rework. One final thought, broken-record time, the result of all in-process acceptance activities, shall be what? Documented – right answer!

Final Acceptance Activities

The FDA no longer requires final acceptance activities. Dr. D is just kidding. Final acceptance activities are considerably more complex than receiving or in-process acceptance activities (Dr. D's opinion). Upon completion of final acceptance, the device manufacturer is basically certifying that the finished medical device meets all requirements (product specification, market specification, etc.) and will be safe and effective for its intended use. Once all of the physical inspection and testing activities have been completed, the entire documentation package assembled as part of the manufacturing process, a.k.a. the Device History Record (DHR) needs to be reviewed. In short, successful completion of the manufacturing process requires verification that finished devices were assembled, inspected, and tested in accordance with the requirements delineated within the Device Master Record (DMR). Until the final review process is completed, all finished devices or batches of finished devices shall be placed into a quarantine area and held until the review has been successfully completed. As part of the final review process, the following activities need to occur.

1. As previously stated, all manufacturing, inspection, and testing requirements, identified within the DMR, must be completed.

2. All of the documentation and data collected and placed into the DHR must be reviewed for acceptability.

3. A formal release of the finished devices or batch of devices must occur, including the name and signature of the individual authorizing the release, and the date the release occurred.

4. Product cannot be released for distribution until formal approval has been achieved. Remember, if product sterilization is required, post manufacturing, release cannot occur prior to the completion of sterilization and post-sterilization testing, as required.

Acceptance Records

Keeping with previous themes, the QSR does not specifically state what constitutes an acceptance activity, only broad categories. That is the job of the device manufacturers. Device manufacturers should be very specific, when writing procedures and creating processes, including the identification of inputs, outputs, and the data needing to be collected as part of acceptance activities. With today's state-of-the-art MRP/ERP systems, such as SAP, detailed manufacturing routers can be created that

132

delineate data requirements throughout the entire manufacturing process. Regardless, the requirement is that all data collected, analyzed, and employed for ascertaining device acceptability, as part of the acceptance process, shall be retained. This data (records of acceptance) forms an integral part of the DHR.

What does the QSR require for acceptance records? As a minimum;

1. The identification and description of the acceptance activity performed, e.g., final electrical test;

2. Documenting the date the activity was performed;

3. Documenting the results of the acceptance activities performed; hopefully, pass or fail;

4. The name and signature of the individual performing the activity; and

5. Documenting the list of equipment (name, nomenclature, serial number, etc.) employed as part of the acceptance activity, when appropriate.

820.86 - Acceptance

The first salient concept needing to be grasped, for achieving compliance to this requirement, is the identification "by suitable means the acceptance status of product." Pretty simple–right? The FDA insists that device makers clearly indicate the acceptance status of product, i.e., good versus bad, conforming versus nonconforming, accepted versus rejected, etc. The second salient concept that needs to be understood, in support of achieving compliance, is that acceptance status "shall be maintained." In fact, acceptance status needs to be maintained throughout the entire manufacturing cycle. The expectation is that nonconforming devices be quickly identified, labeled, removed from the manufacturing cycle, quarantined, and assigned a disposition. Dr. D will explore nonconforming product, in the next chapter. The final salient concept needing to be understood is that acceptance status tools, when effectively applied, will help ensure only finished devices that have passed all of their acceptance activities, will be "distributed, used, or installed."

In simplifying the requirement, make sure your organization pursues the following steps:

1. Establishing a proactive approach to line clearance;

2. Ensuring all product, on the manufacturing floor, is properly identified in regards to batch, quantity, and acceptance status;

3. Ensuring all finished devices are properly identified with the appropriate acceptance status;

4. Employing routers that clearly define each manufacturing, test, or inspection operation;

5. Ensuring operators sign off each process sequence delineated within the router, with name and date, as each sequence is completed; and

6. Ensuring all of these activities, including the final acceptance status, is included in the Device History Record (DHR).

Takeaways from Chapter 13

The key takeaways from this chapter are straightforward. For starters, selecting suppliers capable of supporting an effective SSDP can result in a significant reduction in the RI burden, which results in actual fiscal savings being realized by device manufactures. Additionally, employing statistical tools, when performing in-process acceptance activities, can result in additional savings. Furthermore, final acceptance activities must be successfully completed before finished devices can be released for distribution. Moreover, in Dr. D's world, green equates to good and red equates to the opposite of good, or should I say bad. Remember folks, this is not rocket science being presented here, just the fairly mundane task of labeling product to reflect **correct** acceptance status. Finally, there are a few specific pieces of information that require collection and placement into the records supporting acceptance. One final thought – the QSR does not dictate to device manufacturers how receiving, in-process, and final acceptance activities are to be performed; the QSR specifies that these activities (generically) are required.

Chapter 14 – Nonconforming Product

21 CFR, Part 820

Subpart I

Section 820.90

Chapter 14 – Nonconforming Product

In this chapter, the doctor will provide guidance for 21 CFR, Part 820 – Subpart – I, Nonconforming Product, specifically (820.90). The identification and segregation of nonconforming product should be categorized as a mission-critical process within your quality system. Yes, it is a fundamental requirement of the Quality System Regulation (QSR); however, if an organization fails to control nonconforming product, it risks the ire of the agency during one of their friendly visits. Can you say Form 483 observation? Can you say warning letter? Can you say RECALL? I know, there goes Dr. D. throwing around that nasty 6-letter word again. But seriously folks, Dr. D wants to ensure that device manufacturers are never on the receiving end of enforcement action pursued by the FDA, when the agency heaps contumely on you for failing to comply with the requirements delineated within the QSR. Trust me when I say; "enforcement actions are never any fun."

Warning Letter Violations

As depicted in this chapter, the extractions taken from the FDA's Website, violations of 820.90 are plentiful. One of the trends Dr. D has noted as I performed research and collected information for this book, several companies have racked up multiple violations of the QSR, with the end-result being warning letters that are a small book, in their own right. The doctor just does not understand how medical device manufacturers, regardless of size, continue to make the same mistakes. Nineteen (19) observations, as depicted in the second warning letter extraction, borderlines on absurd. Let's not sugarcoat this device manufacturer's compliance issues, 19 observations is a compliance disaster. Regardless, the behavior exhibited by these manufacturers is the failure to comply with DG Rule # 6 – All procedures, work instructions, drawings, specifications, etc. must be written, well-documented, and controlled within a defined document control system. "Failure to establish and maintain procedures" continues to be a common theme. Additionally, for these warning letter recipients, the concept of formal and documented investigations appears to be foreign. Folks, Dr. D will go on record as stating; "identifying a problem or nonconformance is the easy part, while correcting the nonconformance and ensuring a recurrence does not occur takes some significant work." Can you say use your corrective and preventive action (CAPA) system?

Warning Letter One (April 2010)

> ***Observation 3 of 5*** *– Failure to establish and maintain procedures that address the need to evaluate and document an investigation in order to control product that does not conform to specified requirements as required by 21 CFR § 820.90(a). Specifically, your written procedure for Control of Nonconforming Product (Quality System Procedure 8.3, dated March 22, 2004) does not require an evaluation of the need for a documented investigation for nonconforming products.*

Warning Letter Two (April 2010)

> ***Observation 8 of 19*** *– Failure to establish and maintain procedures that address the identification, documentation, evaluation, segregation, and disposition of nonconforming product, as required by 21 CFR 820.90(a). For example, there is no defined method of identifying, documenting and evaluating nonconforming product and any investigation associated with the nonconforming product. Specifically, email correspondence between the dates of June 29 and July 6, 2009, indicate the need to correct a problem with the data entry field on the waterload software version; however, no further documentation is available addressing this issue.*

Quality System Regulation - 21 CFR, Part 820

QSR – Subpart I – Nonconforming Product

Section 820.90 Nonconforming Product

> *(a)Control of nonconforming product. Each manufacturer shall establish and maintain procedures to control product that does not conform to specified requirements. The procedures shall address the identification, documentation, evaluation, segregation, and disposition of nonconforming product. The evaluation of nonconformance shall include a*

determination of the need for an investigation and notification of the persons or organizations responsible for the nonconformance. The evaluation and any investigation shall be documented.

(b)Nonconformity review and disposition. (1) Each manufacturer shall establish and maintain procedures that define the responsibility for review and the authority for the disposition of nonconforming product. The procedures shall set forth the review and disposition process. Disposition of nonconforming product shall be documented. Documentation shall include the justification for use of nonconforming product and the signature of the individual(s) authorizing the use.

(2) Each manufacturer shall establish and maintain procedures for rework, to include retesting and reevaluation of the nonconforming product after rework, to ensure that the product meets its current approved specifications. Rework and reevaluation activities, including a determination of any adverse effect from the rework upon the product, shall be documented in the DHR.

Nonconforming Product

The effective handling of nonconforming product is essential for all device manufacturers. Identifying, removing, investigating, correcting, and verifying are salient steps that need to be completed. Trust Dr. D when I say, "the mishandling of nonconforming product can be costly, result in product withdraws (RECALLS), and invite a surprise visit from the FDA." One of the major failing that I find with most systems created for managing nonconforming product, is the lack of verification; or shall I say 360-degeree approach to managing the process. As the doctor stated earlier, identification is only a small piece to the puzzle. The best guidance Dr. D can offer to the readers is to invest in developing an effective process for managing nonconforming product. The process should include; (a) robust procedures, (b) a well-designed form, (c) a link to CAPA, (d) a clearly-defined process for disposition, (e) the creation of nonconforming-product tags, (f) a segregated storage area (restricted access), (g) instructions for rework; (h) supplier notification or supplier corrective action request (SCAR), if warranted, (i) a policy for returning nonconforming product to the supplier, (j) a Material Review Board (MRB) process, and last but not least (k) a step for the verification of effectiveness.

Control of Nonconforming Product

Dr. D broken-record time – every QSR requirement commences with a procedure. As depicted in the warning letter section, one of the very first things you can expect from the agency, during a friendly visit, is a review of applicable procedures. Having no procedures quickly equates to Form 483 observations, and multiple Form 483 observations equates to a warning letter. The QSR requires, as a minimum, that procedure(s) address; identification, evaluation, segregation, and disposition. Wait a minute Dr. D, in the previous paragraph you were asking for significantly more data and control. That is correct – but here is why. It is the doctor's belief that teaching and preaching compliance is one of the more important goals in Dr. D's life; however, some processes require more than just compliance to be effective. I think the handling of nonconforming product is one of those salient processes requiring more.

The need for an investigation, potentially root-cause analysis, and the notification of the appropriate organizations (internal and external) are required. If the nonconformance is determined to be external, a.k.a., supplier generated, a SCAR should be issued to prevent a recurrence of the nonconformance. Additionally, ensure all SCAR activity is closed with a verification of effectiveness step; otherwise, history will repeat itself. Furthermore, all of these activities shall be documented. Why – "because documented evidence of compliance is your best defense during a friendly visit from the agency."

Nonconformity Review and Disposition

Since the procedure requirement has already been established, Dr. D will focus on authority and disposition. For starters, you should never have manufacturing be the sole authority for providing disposition of nonconforming product. As a minimum, the doctor recommends including, (a) manufacturing, (b) purchasing, (c) quality, (d) supply chain, (e) R & D, (f) manufacturing engineering and (g) quality engineering. Extended reviewers, employed as necessary, can be (a) clinical / medical sciences, (b) marketing, (c) sales, and (d) the cafeteria "just kidding on the cafeteria." Additionally, all dispositions require more than just names; signatures and dates are also needed. Furthermore, Dr. D **<u>STRONGLY RECOMMENDS</u>** that use-as-is (UAI) never be used for Class 3 devices. A UAI disposition implies product does not meet specification and a conveyance is required to accept the product. In short, the nonconforming product now meets a different specification, probably wider. This equates to a design change. Now you can argue with the doctor until the cows come home, but you will never win this argument. My recommendation will always be to rework nonconforming product to print, scrap and remanufacture, or return the nonconforming product to the supplier. The risk is just too high. Finally, document the results. Why? Broken-record time; "because documented evidence of compliance is your best defense during a friendly visit from the agency."

Rework

Rework of nonconforming product is an area where I see device manufacturers often getting themselves into trouble. You already know Dr. D's position on UAI. That said - rework, which means reworking nonconforming product to established and approved specifications, is a viable option. That said, device manufacturers should not exhibit reckless insouciance (look-it up time) about the rework process. As part of the rework process, the agency's expectation is that the product be retested and/or reevaluated to ensure compliance to the product's <u>approved specification</u> is achieved. If the current product specification is not approved or has been changed and not approved, your organization has other issues. These issues will quickly be exacerbated when the agency visits. Remember design and process changes to Class 3 product will require an FDA review and approval. Can you say 30-day PMA Supplement?

Additionally, the reworked product needs to be assessed for potential long-term impact to product performance, a.k.a., product safety and efficacy. What? For example, let say a finished-device lot has been sterilized employing Ethylene Oxide (EO). While attempting to load the finished devices onto a truck for shipment to distribution a forklift driver (true story) has managed to attack a pallet containing the product with the forklift. As part of the disposition, it has been determined the product will be inspected, repackaged, submitted to EO sterilized a second time, and released for distribution. If the finished devices were only validated for one sterilization cycle (1X), you now have a problem. That is why all aspects of the rework need to be evaluated. Furthermore, all rework activities shall be documented and placed into the Device History Record (DHR).

Finally, Dr. D recommends the DHR be maintained in a pristine condition as accuracy counts. Trust me, the FDA will look at your DHRs and use the review as a stepping-off point for their inspection. Remember, the DHR contains the entire manufacturing history for each device or lot of finished devices. Finally, a complete and accurate DHR is extremely important; "because documented evidence of compliance is your best defense during a friendly visit from the agency."

Takeaways from Chapter 14

The key takeaways from this chapter are: (a) procedures, procedures, and more procedures, (b) understand the importance and elements of effective control of nonconforming product, (c) refrain from the UAI disposition, (d) rework to approved specifications is important, and (e) DHR accuracy counts. If nonconforming product is not effectively controlled, market withdraws should be expected. If the FDA shows up at your doorstep unannounced, due to a **Class 1 or Class 2 RECALL**, well that should not be a real surprise.

Chapter 15 – Corrective and Preventive Action

21 CFR, Part 820

Subpart J

Section 820.100

Chapter 15 – Corrective and Preventive Action

In this chapter, Dr. D will provide guidance for 21 CFR, Part 820 – Subpart – J, Corrective and Preventive Action (CAPA), specifically (820.100). It is Dr. D's personal belief and strong opinion (yes - all of the doctor's opinions are strong), the importance of an effective CAPA system equates to the basic blocking and tackling skills exhibited by good football teams. Additionally, the FDA will always take a quick peek at CAPA during one of their friendly visits. I am sorry, the doctor just mislead the readers. Correction - the FDA will take a long-hard look at CAPA during one of their visits; and use the results as a starting point for their investigation. Furthermore, CAPA should actually result in a problem being permanently resolved or a potential problem averted. Finally, ensure each step of the CAPA process is well-defined. Dr. D recommends pursuing a 5-Step Model encompassing; (a) problem definition, analysis, and scope, (b) initial investigation, (c) problem solution and implementation, (d) verification of effectiveness, and (e) disseminating the results, including management review. Remember to keep in mind the potential impact to product safety and efficacy, regulatory compliance, and overall quality system effectiveness, resulting from CAPA driven changes to product, processes, and procedures.

Warning Letter Violations

As with the previous chapters, the warning-letter issues identified in this chapter expose the lack of procedures and/or effective procedures. Device manufacturers not having written procedures continues to be a salient thread linking compliance issues and violations. The two warning-letter recipients highlighted in this chapter are no exception, and as far as Dr. D is concerned, that is a problem. I am at a loss as to how to motivate device manufacturers to understand and grasp two basic concepts:

1. DG Rule # 1 - compliance to regulations is not optional it is mandatory and dictated by law; and

2. DG Rule # 6 - all procedures, work instructions, drawings, specifications, etc. must be written, well-documented, and controlled within a defined document control system.

What concerns Dr. D greatly is that the medical device industry is expanding rapidly in an effort to keep with an aging population. Let's face it boomers, we are not getting any younger. However, ongoing compliance to the QSR continues to be a growing problem, as evidenced by the significant increase in the issuance of warning letters. Maybe making this book a mandatory reading assignment for device manufacturers (maybe - Devine Guidance – 101) could help stem the flow of current and future compliance problems. Yes, the doctor is delusional. Forcing offending device manufacturers to read this book is probably not going to happen, but Dr. D just cannot help himself as I have never been accused of being a milquetoast (look-it up if you must).

Warning Letter One (August 2010)

> ***Observation 1 of 2*** *– Failure to establish and maintain procedures for implementing corrective and preventive actions, as required by 21 CFR 820.100(a). Specifically, although product quality problems were identified and corrections were made associated with Correction Removal numbers 9 and 10, the corrective action reports were not generated for these corrections and associated activities as specified by SOP 1401 Revision B.*

Warning Letter One (FDA Response) – *We have reviewed your response dated March 31, 2010, and have concluded that the adequacy of the response cannot be determined at this time. Your firm states that SOP 1401 Rev B will be revised, employees retrained, etc., but the firm did not provide copies of the revised procedure and did not provide evidence that employees had received training on the revised procedure because the promised corrective actions had not occurred at the time of the firm's response.*

Warning Letter Two (July 2010)

Observation 1 of 5 – *Failure to establish and maintain procedures for implementing corrective and preventive actions, as required by 21 CFR § 820.100(a). For example, you do not have a written corrective and preventive action procedure.*

Warning Letter Two (FDA Response) – *We have reviewed your response and have concluded that it is inadequate. Your firm has not adequately addressed the requirements of 21 CFR § 820.100(a) nor have you informed us of any specific plan or provided evidence of immediate corrections and systemic corrective actions.*

Quality System Regulation - 21 CFR, Part 820

QSR – Subpart J – Corrective and Preventive Action

Section 820.100 Corrective and Preventive Action

(a) Each manufacturer shall establish and maintain procedures for implementing corrective and preventive action. The procedures shall include requirements for:

(1) Analyzing processes, work operations, concessions, quality audit reports, quality records, service records, complaints, returned product, and other sources of quality data to identify existing and potential causes of nonconforming product, or other quality problems. Appropriate statistical methodology shall be employed where necessary to detect recurring quality problems;

(2) Investigating the cause of nonconformities relating to product, processes, and the quality system;

(3) Identifying the action(s) needed to correct and prevent recurrence of nonconforming product and other quality problems;

(4) Verifying or validating the corrective and preventive action to ensure that such action is effective and does not adversely affect the finished device;

(5) Implementing and recording changes in methods and procedures needed to correct and prevent identified quality problems;

(6) Ensuring that information related to quality problems or nonconforming product is disseminated to those directly responsible for assuring the quality of such product or the prevention of such problems; and

(7) Submitting relevant information on identified quality problems, as well as corrective and preventive actions, for management review.

(b) All activities required under this section, and their results, shall be documented.

Procedures

As evidenced by the two warning-letter excerpts selected for this chapter, procedures for CAPA are required and they need to be effective. When designing and implementing an approach to CAPA, the QSR is very descriptive in regards to what elements are required to be addressed. The QSR specifically calls out seven (7) salient points that shall be addressed in an effective CAPA procedure. Yes, Dr. D presented a 5-Step Model in the introduction; however, the doctor has taken professional liberty and combined a couple of steps. In fact, device manufacturers have the freedom to tailor their approach to CAPA, to fit their specific business model, providing compliance to all of the QSR requirements is achieved.

Analysis

So what is the FDA looking for in regards to analysis? In short, the FDA wants device manufacturers to continually monitor all aspect of their operation and use the results, if warranted, as quality inputs into the CAPA system. For example, unfavorable trends in yields discovered on the manufacturing floor, a nonconformance discovered during an internal quality audit, returned product, and product complaints are a few examples of quality inputs requiring input into the CAPA system. The QSR specifically adds a callout for "other sources of data" and "other quality problems." These catchall phrases equate to considering all potential and actual quality problems for inclusion into the CAPA system or an "all-encompassing approach." Remember two of the salient purposes of CAPA are; (a) to prevent problems from occurring, and (b) prevention of problem recurrence once a problem has occurred.

Investigation

The investigation piece associated with CAPA is pretty cut and dry. The QSR requires device manufacturers to investigate the cause of **ALL** product issues (nonconformities), process issues, and quality system issues. Remember, device manufacturers are not free to pick and choose the problems they want to resolve. Device manufacturers need to fix all nonconformities that have been identified. Additionally, device manufacturers need to exhibit a sense of urgency in executing investigations. One year, or even longer, is just too damned long to complete an initial investigation. Furthermore, if the agency determines the approach to CAPA investigations is unsatisfactory, the device manufacturer can expect a From 483. Finally, please ensure your management representative is contrite as he or she apologizes for your organization's indiscretions and asks the investigator, "Where do I sign the form?" One final comment from Dr. D, ensure the investigation is to root-cause. One area of CAPA investigation, that I continue to see as problematic, is a lack of in-depth analysis capable of resulting in the identification of the real root cause.

Action Identification

The expectation of the FDA is that once a CAPA investigation is complete, the appropriate actions needing to correct nonconformities should be identified. The doctor would like to warn the readers against using too many concessions such as "no-further action is required due to an isolated incident" or an oldie but a goody "no obvious trend."

Device manufacturers that frequently invoke concessions are typically awarded with Form 483s. That said, once the appropriate actions have been identified, Dr. D strongly recommends moving into implementing the recommended actions.

Validation and Verification

Although device manufacturers are typically pretty confident when they move into their implementing solution phase, they must first determine if the proposed action is going to have a negative impact on product safety and efficacy of finished devices. Dr. D is pretty positive, well maybe somewhat positive; device manufacturers do a good job performing in-depth root-cause analysis, while identifying potential corrections to problems. However, the FDA wants device manufacturers to be absolutely sure there is no potential impact to finished devices, prior to implementing changes.

Implementing Solutions

Moving into the implementing-solution phase, device manufacturers need to ensure all changes are documented. Dr. D's not so secret approach is to employ the change request process that feeds the document control system. All changes need to be reviewed and approved. Additionally, changes made to product need to be captured within the Design History File (DHF). Furthermore, ensure FMEAs are reassessed for potential changes in levels of risk and/or occurrences. Finally, all corrections made that change the design or a process associated with a Class 3 device, will probably require a formal review and approval by the FDA. Can you say PMA supplement?

Information Dissemination

Information is and always will be a powerful tool. It should be incumbent upon all device manufacturers to ensure information associated with quality problems, nonconforming product, and potential quality issues be disseminated amongst the proverbial ranks. Successful dissemination of information, i.e., Kaizen circles, etc. will result in the prevention of problem recurrence. For example, if there have been MDRs identifying tip separation from a catheter, and the failure investigation determines the root-cause is process related, the operators on the manufacturing floor need to be made aware of the process problem. Otherwise, trust Dr. D when I say, "history will repeat itself."

Management Review

Ensure CAPA is an integral part of management review. All problems, issues, preventive actions, and corrective actions, shall be incorporated into the management review process. Guess what? If the CAPA system is deemed to be ineffective by the agency, during one of their friendly visits, the ineffectiveness of management responsibility may also come into question. For example, not closing CAPAs on-time, or prolonging closures due to multiple extensions, or claiming a lack of resources to work on CAPAs, will result in two (2) Form 483s observations; one observation written against the CAPA system, and one observation written against management responsibility.

Documentation

Once again, Dr. D must invoke DG Rule # 3 - Document the results of all events in writing, because if it is not documented in writing, the event did not occur. Now climbing onto my soapbox, I will ask you to repeat after Dr. D, "Documented evidence is your best defense during a friendly visit from the FDA." I cannot over emphasize the importance of accurate documentation. Besides, documenting the results is a salient requirement of the QSR.

Takeaways from Chapter 15

I think the most important takeaway, from this chapter, is to use the CAPA system to fix all of your quality problems. A strong CAPA system will allow organizations to track quality problems to closure. Additionally, when problems are identified or potential problems noted, device manufacturers need to act quickly. If you ever want to see Dr. D angry, one way to do it quickly is to place a problem or other nonconformance into the CAPA system; and then take over a year to resolve an issue that should have been corrected in a few days or worst case a couple of weeks. In fact, that type of performance will quickly grab the attention of the agency as well. Remember CAPA is not rocket science. You identify problems and you fix problems.

Chapter 16 – Labeling and Packaging Control

21 CFR, Part 820

Subpart K

Sections 820.120 & 820.130

Chapter 16 – Labeling and Packaging Control

In this chapter, Dr. D will provide guidance for 21 CFR, Part 820 – Subpart – K, Labeling and Packaging Control; specifically 820.120 (Device Labeling) and 820.130 (Device Packaging). Let Dr. D begin this chapter by stating, "Labeling and what constitutes being a label can be confusing for device manufacturers." Labeling, collectively, consists of multiple components, depending on the device manufacturer's packaging configuration. As a minimum, labeling comprises of the outer-most label on a packaged device, the Instructions for Use (IFU), information imbedded into the artwork on a carton or pouch, a pouch label, or even something as benign as a flash label, e.g. "New and Improved." To complicate matters even further, outside of the United States, the Medical Device Directive (MDD) dictates a requirement for labeling to be multi-lingual, e.g., English plus 50 (just kidding – but someday a possible reality). Regardless, the FDA wants to ensure device labeling employed in the United States is clear, concise, legible, and accurate. For example, if a carton label for a catheter depicts a working length of 105 cm, and the actual length of the device is 90 cm, the device manufacturer now has a problem. Can you say, "Misbranded product?" Can you say, "RECALL?" Yes, Dr. D has done it again, throwing around that ugly six-letter word. Seriously, the doctor cannot place enough emphasis on ensuring device labeling is accurate. The doctor has suffered through far too many field actions (code name for RECALLS) due to product labeling issues.

Warning Letter Violations

Dr. D broken-record time again, as this warning-letter extraction reflects another device manufacturer's failure to "establish and maintain procedures." Week after week, violations of the QSR, as evidenced by the warning letters issued by the FDA, reflect a growing trend within the device industry. That trend my friends, continues to be rooted in the lack of procedures required to support compliance with the QSR. It is my personal belief, regardless of regulatory path 510(k), IDE, or PMA, device manufacturers need to have their quality systems reviewed, certified, and approved, by a recognized regulatory body, to circumvent their inerrable (look-it up) policies preventing compliance to the QSR. Now granted, it is my belief the FDA just does not have the resources to accomplish this task of policing, as the number of device manufacturers grows substantially; however, the onus should be placed onto the backs of the device manufacturers to select and pay for a notified body, capable of certifying a quality system. Dr. D is appalled that device manufacturers continue to rack up Form 483 observations and warning letters, while being allowed to distribute devices within the United States. This negative compliance trend needs to be reversed. This reversal will only occur when device manufacturers begin pursuing a veridical (look-it up) approach to compliance.

Warning Letter (February 2010)

> *Observation 3 of 6 – Failure to establish and maintain procedures to control labeling activities, as required by 21 C.F.R. § 820.120. FDA 483 Item 3. Specifically: Your firm has not established written procedures for identifying labeling information, printing and applying labels on the carbon and D1 resin tanks, inspecting the labeling for accuracy, and documenting the labeling inspection results in the device history record. For instance, your firm applies a gray-color label on the mixed-bed resin tanks to prevent mixups with the other resin tanks intended for industrial applications, and a (b)(4) day installation sticker to control bacterial growth in the resin tanks. Your firm has not documented these requirements, and labeling inspections in the batch records (regeneration logs and exchange orders). Another instance, the installation date on the two resin tanks (Tank S/N (b)(4) and (b)(4)) at a hospital occurred a day before the tanks were actually filled at your firm as documented in their batch record.*

Quality System Regulation - 21 CFR, Part 820

QSR – Subpart K – Labeling and Packaging Control

Section 820.120 Device Labeling

Each manufacturer shall establish and maintain procedures to control labeling activities.

(a)Label integrity. Labels shall be printed and applied so as to remain legible and affixed during the customary conditions of processing, storage, handling, distribution, and where appropriate use.

(b)Labeling inspection. Labeling shall not be released for storage or use until a designated individual(s) has examined the labeling for accuracy including, where applicable, the correct expiration date, control number, storage instructions, handling instructions, and any additional processing instructions. The release, including the date and signature of the individual(s) performing the examination, shall be documented in the DHR.

(c)Labeling storage. Each manufacturer shall store labeling in a manner that provides proper identification and is designed to prevent mixups.

(d)Labeling operations. Each manufacturer shall control labeling and packaging operations to prevent labeling mixups. The label and labeling used for each production unit, lot, or batch shall be documented in the DHR.

(e)Control number. Where a control number is required by 820.65, that control number shall be on or shall accompany the device through distribution.

Section 820.130 – Device Packaging

Each manufacturer shall ensure that device packaging and shipping containers are designed and constructed to protect the device from alteration or damage during the customary conditions of processing, storage, handling, and distribution.

Device Labeling

Dr. D broken-record time again – written procedures are a fundamental requirement for compliance with the QSR, as stated by DG Rule # 6 – All procedures, work instructions, drawings, specifications, etc., must be written, well-documented, and controlled within a defined document control system. The QSR, for device labeling, clearly states, ***"Each manufacturer shall establish and maintain procedures to control labeling activities."*** Frankly, I am not sure how the FDA could make this statement any clearer or easier to understand. Shall, in FDA speak, means the requirement is not

optional, as reflected in the Nike™ commercials, "Just Do It." Establish, in FDA speak,

equates to actually developing a well-documented approach to compliance, a.k.a. written

procedures. Maintain, in FDA speak, delineates the need for device manufacturers to

constantly monitor the effectiveness of their written procedures, review the quality

outputs associated with their written procedure, and revise (as appropriate) to ensure

written procedures continue to be effective. Remember folks, this not rocket science.

Label Integrity

What is the value of a label if it does not remained affixed to a product carton or

pouch during normal distribution conditions? To ensure labels do not fall-off or peel-

back, due to adhesion issues, device manufacturers are expected to qualify their label

stock and validate its use, including adhesion. In fact, device manufacturers should be

validating their entire labeling and packaging schemes employing EN ISO 11607-1:2009,

EN ISO 11607-2:2006, and ISTA-2A principles. Ensuring the label remains affixed is

only part of the problem. The printed information on the label must be accurate, and the

label needs to remain legible throughout the entire distribution cycle; including storage,

handling, and where used. That is why tests, such as the "Sullivan Rub Test," are

important.

Labeling Inspection

Ensuring the correct information makes its way onto the product labeling is

mission critical. The information on the label should reflect key characteristics, as

depicted within the product specification (e.g. working length), user information,

regulatory information (e.g. California Proposition 65), recognized symbols, shelf life, batch number, storage and handling instructions, warning statements (e.g. contains Latex or DEHP), single-use, manufacturing address, country of origin, and any additional information deemed appropriate by the device manufacture and/or mandated by law. Although the QSR is US centric, unless you plan on developing special labeling for markets outside of the United States, e.g. the European Union (EU), Dr. D strongly recommends that EN 980:2008, CE Marks, Language Requirements, the use of SI Units, etc., be considered when creating product labeling. Additionally, the doctor recommends a robust approach to the label content review and approval process to ensure label content is accurate. For new product approvals, the FDA will want to review the labeling as part of the initial submission, as will the notified bodies in the EU. Once the label information is deemed accurate, a label specification can be approved and a copy placed in the labeling and boxing area located on the manufacturing floor. Why? Read the next paragraph.

The approved label specification can be employed by the quality organization or designee for label inspection. The QSR clearly states, "***Labeling shall not be released for storage or use until a designated individual(s) has examined the labeling for accuracy.***" As part of determining label accuracy, the information depicted on the label, the legibility of information depicted on the label, and the quantity of labels received, printed, and retained needs to be verified. Evidence of this verification step shall be retained in the Device History Record (DHR), including (a) the signatures of the individuals performing the inspection, and (b) the date the inspection was performed. A copy of the printed label should also be retained in the DHR. Dr. D recommends creating a label inspection sheet so a copy of the label can be affixed to the backside of the sheet for retention purposes.

Labeling Storage

Labeling storage begins with batch numbers assigned to the label stock, pre-printed labels, flash labels (Dr. D hates flash labels, as their use is difficult to control), etc. Employing effective line clearance in the labeling area will result in the prevention of potential label mix-ups. Dr. D. has witnessed the perils associated with an operator loading the wrong label stock onto a Zebra Xiii Printer (no Dr. D is not a paid spokesperson for Zebra), the labels subsequently printed and affixed to the cartons of finished medical devices, and the devices placed into distribution. Can you say RECALL? Yes, there goes Dr. D invoking that nasty six-letter word again - stop. As stated in the previous paragraph, it is important to keep track of the number of labels printed. In a perfect world, an automated approach to printing and affixing labels is preferred; however, because of the varying sizes of labels, pouches, cartons, and the expense associated with automation, many manufacturers still apply the labels manually.

Labeling Operations

It is the strong opinion of Dr. D, "There is no better way to control mix-ups on the production floor then to employ an effective approach to line clearance." The foundation for effective line clearance is the batch control of materials, i.e., labels, pouches, IFUs, and cartons. Obviously, all of the batch information associated with labeling and packaging shall be retained in the DHR, as should a copy of the label, as previously stated. Another key influencer affecting line clearance, as with all manufacturing and inspection operations is employee training. Remember, pouching, boxing, and labeling are the final manufacturing steps prior to finished devices shipping to sterilization and distribution. The quality and manufacturing staff working in the labeling and boxing area must possess a keen eye for detail and be thoroughly trained in the execution of their duties.

Control Numbers

As part of the control number requirement, the QSR invokes 820.65. Section 820.65 of the QSR, is the requirement for traceability. When the use of a control number is required by regulation, e.g., surgical implant, the assigned control number must remain with the finished device or devices throughout their entire life cycle. The entire life cycle concludes with the use of the device(s), or the scrapping of the device(s) – in short, the device is no longer in service and available for use. It does not end with the sale. Remember, traceability should be a salient requirement. Device manufacturers will rely heavily on traceability, should a RECALL ever become necessary. I know, stop with the "R-Word" already.

Device Packaging

Dr. D has already expounded on the virtues of validating packaging schemes to ensure finished medical devices are adequately protected during the trials and tribulations associated with, as the QSR states, "customary conditions of processing, storage, handling, and distribution. Device manufacturers can have pretty boxes, eye-catching color schemes, and flash labels fit for use on laundry-soap cartons; however, none of these is worth a hill of beans if the packaging does not prevent damage to the device, or the sterile barrier. That said, device manufacturers must validate packaging and the effectiveness of the packaging for protecting the finished medical device. The expectation of the FDA and regulatory bodies around the world is that the packaging validation include packaged product:

1. That has been processed through the appropriate sterilization cycle (if applicable);

2. Exposed to a reasonable distribution challenge (ISTA-2A); and

3. Supported by aging studies to support shelf-life (accelerated to support initial product approval followed by real-time).

Packaging is an extremely important deliverable as part of the overall product design cycle. Remember, regardless of how good a device design might be; it is worthless if the device cannot be delivered to healthcare professionals ready for use. Device safety and device efficacy trumps speed to market any day of the week.

Takeaways from Chapter 16

There are three takeaways from this chapter. One – the accuracy of device labeling is a mission-critical step for device manufacturers. If the information depicted on a device label is incorrect, device manufactures can expect to withdraw product from market (note – Dr. D did not use the word RECALL). Two – ensure product packaging and labeling are properly validated, including distribution cycles, storage conditions, and useable shelf life. Three – if product is going to be distributed outside of the United States, become familiar with the MDD and EN 980. Designing labeling schemes for deployment in multiple markets can result in significant cost saving.

Chapter 17 – Handling, Storage, Distribution, and Installation

21 CFR, Part 820

Subpart L

Sections 820.140, 820.150, 820.160, & 820.170

Chapter 17 – Handling, Storage, Distribution, and Installation

In this chapter, Dr. D will provide guidance for 21 CFR, Part 820, Subpart – L (Handling, Storage, Distribution, and Installation). Have you ever had the misfortune of ordering an item, over the Internet, having it shipped to your home, and upon opening the box, find the item badly damaged? Let's face it ladies and gentlemen, regardless of the carrier, USPS, UPS, or Fed-X, products take a beating during the rigors of "routine shipping and handling." Back in April of 2010, Dr. D was about to be the proud owner of a new 57" flat-screen television. The second my eyes focused on the condition of the shipping container, I knew I was going to have issues. Sure enough, the screen was shattered. The moral of the story is that the packaging scheme employed by the manufacturer was not suitable for a routine distribution environment, regardless of potential handling issues. Now granted, receiving a damaged TV and waiting for the replacement is nothing more than a minor inconvenience; however, medical devices not so minor. The expectation of healthcare providers is that the procured medical device is useable, right out of the box, while being safe and effective during its intended use. If the device does not work, the device manufacturer will receive a complaint. If it is determined that a damaged device has resulted in patient injury or death, the device manufacturer can expect to receive a Form 3500A (Mandatory Reporting for an adverse event). This form is required by law as part of the FDA's Medical Device Reporting (MDR) process. Receive enough of these forms (a.k.a., MDRs); the device manufacturer can expect a visit from the agency.

Warning Letter Violations

The first warning letter observation falls into the category of the proverbial truth in labeling category. The labeling must be accurate. No doubt pursuing a Sisyphean (look-it up) a task such as providing obviously inaccurate handling information, on the label, is problematic for this device manufacturer; however, it can be quickly resolved. The device manufacturer, depicted in the first warning letter can; (a) commence delivering devices via the Good Humor Ice Cream Truck, keeping the storage temperature between two (2) and 8-degrees Celsius; (b) correct the labeling to reflect the proper handling and storage conditions; (c) actually test the packaging scheme and determine the appropriate handling and storage information; or (d) answers b and c. If you choose answer d, you have successfully comprehended the material presented in this book by Dr. D.

Now the second warning letter recipient has simply failed to invoke DG Rule # 6 – All procedures, work instructions, drawings, specifications, etc. must be written, well-documented, and controlled within a defined document control system. Remember ladies and gentlemen, in the medical device industry, compliance to the QSR is mandatory and dictated by Federal Code (a.k.a., **LAW**) not optional (DG Rule # 1). Dr. D broken-record time, all aspects of a device manufacturer's quality/business system shall be defined by procedures.

Damn, Dr. D is really growing tired of surfing the FDA database on warning letters and finding the constant barrage of observations commencing with; *"Failure to establish and maintain procedures."* The garrulous pose depicted in these observations point to the same conclusion, repeatedly. Can you guess what that conclusion might be? If you said a lack of, or missing procedures, you would be correct. Device manufacturers, please read the QSR. Device manufacturers please generate written procedures to support compliance to the QSR. Device manufactures please, please, and pretty please, understand that compliance to the QSR is not optional, it is mandated by law. Dr. D would like to opine that all chapters of this book are worthy of reading, although I strongly suggest reading chapter one, and brushing up on the doctor's rules. In this case, DG Rule # 1 - Compliance to regulations is not optional, it is mandatory and dictated by law is quite appropriate.

Additionally, the 19 observations awarded to the owner of the third warning letter extraction is unacceptable. Where in the @#$* is the management representative for quality. The doctor is going to assume, this individual was meeting with his or her tailor for a custom-fitted orange jumpsuit. Can you say consent decree? As for the second warning letter, this device manufacturer should not take solace in knowing they received only nine (9) observations. That is still way too many observations. Maybe the management representatives from these manufacturers share the same tailor (sorry – just some bad humor from Dr. D). At the end of the day, the truth in labeling becomes a major factor in this second warning letter observation. If the manufacturer's specification (product spec) delineates specific storage requirements, these requirements, after being substantiated through testing, need to make their way onto the labeling. Otherwise, how can this device manufacturer guarantee the expected performance requirements for product shelf life were achieved?

Warning Letter One (November 2009)

> ***Observation 2 of 5*** *– Failure to ensure that deterioration or other adverse effects to product do not occur, as required by 21 CFR § 820.140. Specifically, the labeling for all media states to store the product at 2°C to 8°C. Your firm does not ship the product at 2°C to 8°C as required by the labeling and has no justification documented for shipping the product under non-refrigerated conditions.*

Warning Letter Two (May 2010)

Observation 9 of 12 – Failure to establish and maintain adequate procedures that describe the methods for authorizing receipt from and dispatch to storage areas and stock rooms, as required by 21 CFR 820.150(b). Specifically, you have no procedure in place to specify who is authorized to retrieve mini-batches of product found in Room (b)(4).

FDA Response to Observation 9 of 12 – We have reviewed your response and concluded that it is not adequate because although you stated that you will create a procedure for controlling in-process materials in Room. You did not provide a copy of the procedure for FDA's review.

Observation 10 of 12 – Failure to establish and maintain adequate procedures for the control of storage areas and stock rooms for product to prevent mixups, damage, deterioration, contamination, or other adverse effects pending use or distribution and to ensure that no obsolete, rejected, or deteriorated product is used or distributed, as required by 21 CFR 150(a). For example, the mini-batch materials (optimized gold/membrane combinations) stored in Room (b)(4) are labeled "quarantine"; however, these materials are used to manufacture product.

FDA Response to Observation 10 of 12 – Your response to this observation appears to be adequate.

Warning Letter Three (March 2010)

Observation 12 of 19 – Failure to establish and maintain procedures for control and distribution of finished devices to ensure that only those devices approved for release are distributed and to maintain distribution records which include or refer to the location of (1) the name and address of the initial consignee; (2) the identification and quantity of devices shipped; (3) the date shipped; and (4) any control number(s) used, as required by 21 CFR 820.160. For example, when requested, procedures for controlling and distributing finished devices and distribution records for products released into distribution for 2008 and 2009 were not provided.

Warning Letter Four (August 2009)

Observation 6 of 9 – Failure to assure that you have not distributed devices that have deteriorated beyond acceptable fitness for use as required by 21 CFR 820.160(a). For example, one of the components used in manufacturing hundreds of different products in the "Ultralite" line including different variations of colostomy, urostomy and ileostomy pouches is at (b)(4). According to the manufacturer's specifications for this product (b)(4), the component has a 3 year shelf life when stored at 70 F, 50% relative humidity and out of direct sunlight. You used this information to establish and label a 3 year shelf life for their products, but you did not include a temperature or humidity requirement on your label and have not performed any in-house validation activities to support the expiration date of the products.

Quality System Regulation - 21 CFR, Part 820

QSR – Subpart L – Handling, Storage, Distribution, and Installation

Section 820.140 Handling

Each manufacturer shall establish and maintain procedures to ensure that mixups, damage, deterioration, contamination, or other adverse effects to product do not occur during handling.

Section 820.150 – Storage

(a) Each manufacturer shall establish and maintain procedures for the control of storage areas and stock rooms for product to prevent mixups, damage, deterioration, contamination, or other adverse effects pending use or distribution and to ensure that no obsolete, rejected, or deteriorated product is used or distributed. When the quality of product deteriorates over time, it shall be stored in a manner to facilitate proper stock rotation, and its condition shall be assessed as appropriate.

(b) Each manufacturer shall establish and maintain procedures that describe the methods for authorizing receipt from and dispatch to storage areas and stock rooms.

Section 820.160 Distribution

(a) Each manufacturer shall establish and maintain procedures for control and distribution of finished devices to ensure that only those devices approved for release are distributed and that purchase orders are reviewed to ensure that ambiguities and errors are resolved before devices are released for distribution. Where a device's fitness for use or quality deteriorates over time, the procedures shall ensure that expired devices or devices deteriorated beyond acceptable fitness for use are not distributed.

(b) Each manufacturer shall maintain distribution records which include or refer to the location of:

(1) The name and address of the initial consignee;

(2) The identification and quantity of devices shipped;

(3) The date shipped; and

(4) Any control number(s) used.

Section 820.170 – Installation

(a) Each manufacturer of a device requiring installation shall establish and maintain adequate installation and inspection instructions, and where appropriate test procedures. Instructions and procedures shall include directions for ensuring proper installation so that the device will perform as intended after installation. The manufacturer shall distribute the instructions and procedures with the device or otherwise make them available to the person(s) installing the device.

(b) The person installing the device shall ensure that the installation, inspection, and any required testing are performed in accordance with the manufacturer's instructions and procedures and shall document the inspection and any test results to demonstrate proper installation.

Handling

Once the device manufacturer has validated a packaging scheme capable of surviving the rigors of normal and sometimes not so normal distribution channels, the correct device must make it into the hands of the physicians. Sounds pretty simple right? Wrong! Device manufacturers can write and train to procedures that support effective handling practices. Device manufacturers can successfully validate packaging schemes. However, without effective line-clearance practices in place and adequate final inspection, the potential for device mix-ups will occur. Trust Dr. D when I say; "Murphy is always lurking in the corner." If the device, entering into the distribution cycle, is placed into the wrong package or affixed with the incorrect label, you can expect to invoke an exercise in the ancient art of RECALL. Yes, I said it, that nasty 6-letter word, RECALL, RECALL, and RECALL!

Not wanting to end the handling aspect on a sour note, good handling practices, including effective line clearance, accurate label information in regards to handling and storage, can be successfully implemented with well-written procedures, training, validation testing, and sustained vigilance by all. Over the years, I have always taught my direct reports to handle medical devices with great care. Why? Because the recipient of the therapy provided by one of these devices could very easily be a family member. In fact, it just might be you.

Storage

Similar to the handling requirement, device manufacturers, ***"shall establish and maintain procedures for the control of storage areas and stock rooms for product to prevent mix-ups, damage, deterioration, contamination, or other adverse effects."*** The caveat here is that the environment and location comes into play versus just the handling. For example, if the storage temperature requirement, depicted in the first warning letter were a valid requirement, the devices would need to be stored in that cold environment with evidence of effective temperature control. One of Dr. D's favorite storage requirements, as placed on labeling is, **"Store in a Cool Dark Place."** I guess that means storing devices in the Bat Cave is an option. Remember – if storage information on the label, e.g., temperature, has not been validated, it should not be on the device label. What the agency is really searching for, when evaluating the storage requirement, is assurances device manufactures are not shipping damaged, discrepant, or expired devices into distribution.

Additionally, if devices have the potential for performance degradation, while sitting on the shelf in a distribution center, stock room, or similar environment, the devices shall be adequately protected from damage and the influences of the environment. For example, if a polymer is employed in a catheter shaft, and exposure to UV light can accelerate the breakdown of molecular chains; then special packaging (recommended foil pouches) and other protective steps should be employed. Regardless, the storage life for finished medical devices shall be determined through validation testing and the results documented. Remember, the useable shelf life is important data that will need to be placed onto the label of the finished medical device.

Another important aspect of device storage is stock rotation. With a variety of ERP and MRP systems readily available, e.g., SAP™ (no Dr. D is not a paid spokesperson for SAP), batch management, including expiration dates, can be assigned and controlled systemically. In fact, once an expiration date is reached, an electronic gate should keep product from shipping. Dr. D strongly suggests adding at least a 3-month buffer to the expiration date and potentially longer, premised on inventory turns. Your supply chain folks can help make that determination.

Equally important, in regards to storage location, is the access and responsibilities of individuals being granted access. The FDA feels so strongly about the control of product entering and leaving the stock rooms, they require device manufacturers to create procedures to delineate the practices for authorizing material receipts and material being dispatched to storage locations and stock rooms. The message that really needs to be understood is that all aspects of handling and storage must be effectively controlled. You can take it to the proverbial bank, when the FDA arrives on your doorstep for a friendly visit, they will spend time in the stock room. There are two ways to make a lasting first impression. The first, have the stockroom in complete disarray with clear evidence of ineffective inventory control and poor handling and storage techniques. The reward for this effort is simple. Can you say Form 483? The alternative is to have a well-organized, and clean stock room, with every item in the room identified, with a batch number, expiration date (if appropriate), part number, etc. Remember, a first impression, regardless of the path chosen, is a lasting impression.

Distribution

"Each manufacturer shall establish and maintain procedures for control and distribution of finished devices." This quote is right out of the QSR and is invoked throughout the entire QSR. That said, how could device manufacturers fail to have written procedures? As delineated within 820.160, the FDA wants to ensure device manufacturers release only approved devices for distribution. Additionally, the FDA wants to ensure adequate review and diligence is pursued in regards to filling purchase orders. If device manufacturers really want to endear themselves to their customer base, ship the wrong product to a doc. Even better, go on backorder and not have a device to ship, a.k.a., helping the competition. Better yet, ship a product that has or will shortly reach end-of-life, a.k.a., expired shelf life. Furthermore (broken-record time), all product shelf life should be validated through testing; accelerated aging to get the product to market and real-time aging to substantiate the results. If a device manufacturer has not performed aging studies, the product should not be released for sale and distribution. Can you say RECALL? Yes, once again Dr. D has invoked the curse of that nasty 6-letter word.

Records

Broken-record time again, no pun intended, documented evidence (records) is always a device manufacturer's best defense during a friendly visit by the agency. Remember, FDA visits are investigations not audits. The evidence collected during these investigations can be employed in support of further enforcement or potential criminal action against device manufacturers. That said, some of the records requiring to be retained in support of medical device distribution are:

1. The name and address of the initial consignee (Dr. D. also strongly recommends a telephone number and point of contact – just in case a recall becomes necessary);

2. Device part numbers, quantity shipped, batch numbers, serial numbers, etc.;

3. The date the product shipped (Dr. D also recommends recording the carrier and method of shipment, tracking numbers, waybill numbers, etc.); and

4. Control numbers employed (as appropriate.

Installation

"Each manufacturer of a device requiring installation shall establish and maintain adequate installation and inspection instructions, and where appropriate test procedures." Once again, extracted right out of the QSR, the need for instructions and procedures is clearly depicted. Now typically, installation is a task associated with capital equipment, e.g., cardiac ablation system; however, the personnel in the Catheter Lab are not just going to power up the system and allow the attending physician to ablate away. The expectation is that an established protocol, hopefully in the operator's manual or Instructions for Use (IFU), is going to be comprehended and followed. It is up to device manufacturers to ensure this information is available and accurate. Additionally, the installation and use information should accompany the piece of equipment or device, as the QSR specifically requires these instructions to be available to personnel performing the installation. Furthermore, if a finished medical device (e.g., disposable catheter) is to be integrated with a piece of capital equipment, the IFU needs to be available to ensure the overall installation; capital equipment, disposable device, and other ancillary devices, if appropriate are correctly installed prior to their use.

Documentation

Once again, record keeping, a.k.a., documentation, is important. For starters, Dr. D strongly suggests that individuals performing the installation be adequately trained and the training documented. Additionally, once installation has been successfully completed, the results, test, inspection, etc. shall be documented. Another key component of the installation process is to ensure these records, where appropriate, make their way back to the device history record (DHR).

When dealing with capital equipment, configuration and configuration control are critical pieces of information needed to support servicing. For example, if a software, firmware, or hardware change is required as part of a refurbishment effort, understanding the current configuration, while ensuring all proposed changes have been made is an extremely critical process. The last thing a field-service technician wants to see in the field is an old piece of equipment missing previously required upgrades. A device manufacturer that fails miserably in the fine art of configuration control can expect to experience the pain associated with a RECALL.

Takeaways from Chapter 17

For this chapter, Dr. D will step down from the soapbox and not preach about the importance of written procedures and documented evidence. That said, there are multiple takeaways from this chapter. For starters, the accuracy of handling and storage information, depicted on labeling, affixed to medical devices, should be considered mission critical. As depicted in the warning letter extractions, inaccurate handling and storage information was cited, as an observation, in a warning letter. If a device manufacturer does not require the storage or shipment of product at a specific temperature, they should not place specific temperature information on the device label.

Secondly, effective and robust handling and storage processes, for medical devices, need to be sustained throughout the entire distribution cycle. Shipping expired product or damaged product is unacceptable. That is why the FDA holds device manufacturers to task in regards to the proper validation of device packaging schemes, capable of surviving routine and not so routine handling and storage practices, including the potential influences for adverse environmental conditions. Thirdly, distribution and installation are extremely important processes that ensure approved, safe, and effective medical devices make it into the hands of healthcare practitioners. There is no point in designing and developing devices if manufacturers fail at effectively executing these salient tasks. Dr. D will jump back onto his soapbox and emphatically state; "You need written procedures to participate in the medical device industry, it is part of the price of admission." In fact, if there are no written procedures; it is Dr. D's humble opinion; "no quality system exists."

Chapter 18 – Records

21 CFR, Part 820

Subpart M

Sections 820.180, 820.181, 820.186, & 820.198

Chapter 18 - Records

In this chapter, Dr. D will provide guidance for 21 CFR, Part 820, Subpart – M (Records). Yes, the doctor understands that general requirements are boring; however, just like basic blocking and tackling drills in football, device manufacturers must get the basics correct. If you want to watch an FDA investigator scintillate (look-it-up if you must) during a friendly visit, fail to execute in regards to the basic requirements depicted throughout the Quality System Regulation (QSR). Even better, present the investigator with a farrago (look-it-up) of policies and procedures, and dare to call it a cohesive quality system. In fact, Dr. D dares you to do so.

Warning Letter Violations

It is a salient requirement to consider the importance of records while understanding that fundamentally sound record accuracy and retention practices equates to having a reasonable defense in regards to claiming compliance to the QSR. Dr. D scoured through a significant number of warning letter and observations in support of this chapter. Dr. D finds the large number of offending device manufacturers appalling.

The first warning-letter recipient, documented in this chapter, discarded the inspection checklist after each device was shipped. WHAT WERE THEY THINKING? HELLO! For starters, what is the purpose of employing a documented checklist if it is discarded after shipment? Remember the world is going green; and now we have a device manufacturer killing trees for no apparent reason. Obviously, the documenting of final acceptance activities and the retention of the results, pass or fail, is considered documented evidence and a salient requirement of the QSR. Once the only evidence is tossed into the circular file by this manufacturer, there is no evidence the inspection ever occurred. This is a clear violation of the QSR, in which case, this device manufacturer was appropriately rewarded with a Form 483 and subsequent warning letter. It was also a violation of DG Rule # 3 - Document the results of all events in writing, because if it is not documented in writing, the event did not occur.

Dr. D was able to locate multiple warning-letter observations, highlighting the lack of understanding of the DMR requirement resulting in documented non-compliances. Once again, after reading the observations, the warning letters were clearly justified. The second violator failed to ensure all of the appropriate records, such as device specifications and production processes, were identified for inclusion into the DMR. It is the doctor's opinion; this observation was rooted in one of my favorite compliance issues, "failure to establish written procedures." If this device manufacturer adhered to DG Rule # 6 – All procedures, work instructions, drawings, specifications, etc. must be written, well-documented, and controlled within a defined document control system; the observation could have been averted.

For those of you that have made it through most of this book, the third warning-letter recipient should be quite familiar to you by now. The 19 observations are a dead giveaway. In fact, as my favorite comedian Carlos Mencia would say, "Duh, duh-duh." In general, the agency was thoroughly impressed with all aspects of this device manufacturer's approach to compliance (just kidding of course). In reality, the inspection resulted in two specific observations against 820.181. Not only was there an issue with the overall approach to compiling and sustaining DMR's; when requested, specifications that should reside in the DMR could not be produced. Dr. D broken-record time again, if there is no documented evidence, i.e., specification, report, etc. the event never occurred.

If there is no evidence available to provide the FDA, during an inspection; not only did the event not occur, the offending device manufacturer should be prepared to receive a Form 483.

In this fourth warning letter, the offending device manufacturer has failed to include all records associated with the manufactured device into the DHR. Besides, being the recipient of a 10-observation warning letter, "duh duh-duh," they failed to incorporate packaging and labeling steps into the DHR. Remember, packaging and labeling are key operations incorporated into the manufacturing process. In fact, the part numbers and lot numbers associated with the packaging and labeling operations need to be captured in the DHR. Typically, the packaging and labeling steps are embedded in the production routers. Additionally, a copy of the actual printed label and DFU, packaged with the product, should be retained in the DHR.

Furthermore, when responding to a warning letter or Form 483 observation; specifically when the correction will be resolved by modifying a document or work instruction, manufacturers need to send a copy of the actual change to the agency. Why? Because without documented evidence, the event did not occur, or in this case, the change was never made.

As for the fifth warning-letter recipient, this manufacturer continues to be one of the doctor's favorite offending device manufacturers. As Dr. D has stated on multiple occasions, this manufacturer was awarded with a 19-obervation warning letter, with a few dozen subparts. Once again, "Failure to establish and maintain procedures," is a prevalent theme. Please keep in mind, if the device sold is categorized as software, and the software is being distributed, a DHR is required. Additionally, the product shall be labeled and a copy of the labeling retained in the DHR Furthermore, all changes need to be captured. Finally, because Dr. D is always impressed with a device manufacturer that has managed to collect a 19-observation warning letter, the doctor is compelled to shout out an additional "Duh, Duh-Duh."

The recipient of warning-letter six definitely endeared themselves to the agency. Not only was the agency thrilled with the lack of an effective procedure, this was a repeat violation from a previous investigation. The agency clearly did not approve of the written response provided. So overall, strike one (1) was an ineffective procedure. Strike two (2) was a repeat violation. Strike three (3) was an unacceptable response to the agency. In baseball terms (World Series time), these three strikes equate to a strikeout in the eyes of the FDA. Striking out coupled with a 10-observation warning letter equates to this device manufacturer about to enter a very long and interesting relationship with the agency.

The recipients of warning letters seven and eight also failed to establish what the FDA perceives as effective written procedures in support of complaint handling. To make matters worse, the recipient of the third warning letter failed to respond back to the agency within the 15-day timeframe. Give me a break folks; I cannot believe that a device manufacturer would be willing to place their entire organization at risk by failing to respond to the agency within 15-days. What were they thinking?

The warning-letter winner recognized in the ninth slot of this chapter "failed to establish and maintain adequate procedures." Additionally, the recipient of this ominous letter from the agency logged complaints but never investigated the complaints. I guess that would beg Dr. D to ask the question, "What is the point?" Furthermore, what part of, "took care of the issue," can remotely be construed as effective complaint resolution? Hello! Dr. D is absolutely floored that this offending device manufacturer has

failed to pursue any attempt at rudimentary root-cause analysis. "Took care of the issue"

is an acceptable response from the doctor's auto mechanic; however, a device

manufacturer – not so much.

In throwing the proverbial gas onto the fire and fanning the flames, this device

manufacturer also failed to provide a reasonable response to the agency. The poor

response, coupled with the 11-observation warning letter, means this device manufacturer

will remain in the FDA's doghouse for a very long time. Nice!

The tenth warning-letter recipient "failed to establish and maintain procedures."

Once again, Dr. D hopes the readers are connecting the dots and seeing the trend here.

For those of you that are not seeing the trend, please commit to memory Devine

Guidance Rule # 6 – All procedures, work instructions, drawings, specifications, etc.

must be written, well-documented, and controlled with in a defined document control

system.

Warning Letter One (March 2010)

Observation 7 of 7 – *Failure to retain records required by this part for a period of time equivalent to the design and expected life of the device, but in no case less than 2 years from the date of release for commercial distribution by the manufacturer, as required by 21 CFR 820.180(b). For example, your firm documents the final inspection of the Water Lily on a checklist, but discards the checklist after each Water Lily device is shipped.*

FDA Response to Observation 7 of 7 – *We have reviewed your response and have concluded that it is inadequate. Your firm has not adequately addressed the requirements of 21 CFR 820.180(b) nor have you informed us of any specific plan or provided evidence of immediate corrections and systemic corrective actions.*

Warning Letter Two (June 2010)

Observation 4 of 6 – *Failure to maintain device master records (DMR's) as required by 21 CFR § 820.181. Specifically, your firm has not established and maintained DMRs, that include, or refer to the location of the device specifications, production process specifications, quality assurance procedures and specifications, packaging and labeling specifications, and installation, maintenance, and servicing procedures and methods, for its Cranial Orthosis devices.*

Warning Letter Three (March 2010)

Observation 13 of 19 *– Failure to establish and maintain device master records (DMR's), as required by 21 CFR 820.181. For example, when requested, no DMR for the EGGSAS software used in the three 3CPM Electrogastrogram versions: Research, Research Waterload, and Waterload was provided.*

Observation 14 of 19 *– Failure to maintain adequate device master records that include, or refer to the location of, device specifications including appropriate drawings, composition, formulation, component specifications, and software specifications, as required by 21 CFR 820.181(a). For example, when requested, the software specifications for the software update that occurred in **(b)(4)** or the software updates that occurred between **(b)(4)** could not be located.*

Warning Letter Four (September 2010)

Observation 7 of 10 *– The device history record does not demonstrate that the device was manufactured in accordance with 21 CFR 820. Specifically, your device history records for the ME dryers do not include records of the packaging or labeling of the devices as required by 21 CFR 820.184. Packaging and labeling are part of the manufacturing process and all dates of these activities need to be recorded. Furthermore, a copy of the device label, including lot number, must be kept in the device history record.*

FDA Response to Observation 7 of 10 *– Your response states that the "ME Packaging Overview" document will be revised. We cannot make any assessment regarding the corrective actions because no revised document was submitted.*

Warning Letter Five (March 2010)

Observation 15 of 19 *– Failure to establish and maintain procedures to ensure that device history records (DHR) for each batch, lot, or unit are maintained to demonstrate that the device is manufactured in accordance with the device master record and the requirements of 21 CFR Part 820, as required by 21 CFR 810.184. For example:*

    *a. When requested, no DHR for the research, research-waterload or the waterload software Version **(b)(4)** tested and distributed to customers was provided.*
    b. There is no record of device labeling.
    c. Changes to the software are not documented in the Design History File and

are not tracked and/or verified. There is no documentation listing the number and/or type of changes that were made.

Warning Letter Six (September 2010)

Observation 9 of 10 – Procedures for receiving, reviewing, and evaluating complaints by a formally designated unit have not been adequately established as required by 21 CPR 820.198(a). The Customer Complaint and Return Authorization Instructions, RA-WI-001 Revision 00, was insufficient. For example:

i. The procedure did not ensure that complaints were evaluated to determine whether the complaint constituted an event required to be reported under 21 CFR 803, Medical Device Reporting;

ii. The procedure did not require that all complaints were evaluated to determine if an investigation was necessary;

iii. The procedure did not require that when no investigation was conducted, the reason and name of individual responsible for the decision not to investigate was recorded;

iv. The procedure did not require that when a complaint represented an MDR reportable event, that the complaint was promptly reviewed and evaluated by a designated individual and that the subsequent investigation include a determination of whether the device failed to meet specifications, was being used for treatment or diagnosis, and the relationship of the device to the reported event.

FDA Response to Observation 9 of 10 – The same observation was made during the previous inspection of July 2006. Your response included a revised Customer Complaint and Return Authorization Instructions procedure, RA-WI-001, Rev. 01, dated 8/15/10. We cannot determine whether or not the revised procedure and customer complaint form will be satisfactory under actual conditions of use, nor have you provided any evidence that appropriate training has been conducted for all groups listed (quality, sales, customer service, and management) on the revised procedure, and associated requirements and procedures, such as MDR reporting. Furthermore, the response again cites the promised corrective actions regarding management reviews, and as stated previously, we do not consider that response to be sufficient.

Warning Letter Seven (September 2010)

Observation 5 of 5 – Failure to establish and maintain procedures for receiving, reviewing, and evaluating complaints by a formally designated unit, as required by 21 CFR 820.198(a).

Naturalyte Acid Concentrate products:
For example, on June 09, 2009, your company received a complaint (PIR

200901506) regarding a possible dialyzer reaction incident that occurred on April 6, 2009 in which a dialysis patient experienced lose of pulse/consciousness and CPR was required. Related complaint, PIR 200901614 was received on June 10, 2010, and referenced a second occurrence of a possible dialyzer reaction on April 20, 2009 in which the patient loss consciousness again, and required CPR a second time. The patient ultimately died on May 08, 2009 due to coronary artery disease, end stage renal failure, and sepsis.

The second complaint was voided, contrary to your own SOP S100006-01, even though two events were clearly reported. The original complaint file was subsequently closed on July 17, 2009 without investigation to determine that the event was not reportable under 21 CFR Part 803. The file did not include any documentation that your devices did not cause the events described in the two separate incidents. We are concerned that you relied on your own internal assessment to make such a decision, without further investigation or contact with the complainant.

Also, your firm received a complaint on June 23, 2008 (PIR 200801118) involving Naturalyte products (08-4017) which indicated that since the labels look the same, "the wrong product actually has been used on one occasion". The complaint did not include any documentation that indicated an attempt was made to follow-up with the complainant to determine whether a patient reaction was involved.

Warning Letter Eight (September 2010)

Observation 3 of 8 – Failure to establish and maintain adequate procedures for receiving, reviewing, and evaluating complaints by a formally designated unit, as required by 21 CFR 820.198(a). For example, your firm's **(b)(4)** does not state how to receive, review, and evaluate complaints in a timely manner.

FDA Response to Observation 3 of 8 – Your response dated June 14, 2010, was received after the 15 day time frame for consideration; therefore it has not been reviewed at this time.

Warning Letter Nine (October 2010)

Observation 4 of 11 – Failure to establish and maintain adequate procedures for receiving, reviewing, and evaluating complaints by a formally designated unit, as required by 21 CFR 820.198(a). For example, your firm failed to maintain complete complaint records as required by the law. A review of 35 complaints from 2009 and 2010 revealed none of the records met the quality system requirements for complaint files because there was no documentation to show the complaints were investigated and what action was taken following the investigation of the complaints. Listed below is an example of this deficiency of the complaint handling system of your firm:

- A complaint received on May 20, 2009, for the PACS device states, "...she tried merging a patient's studies...But now that she has done that there are no studies under the patient's profile." The problem resolution is documented as ".. . took care of the issue." There is no additional information maintained for this complaint.

- A complaint received on July 10, 2009, for the PACS device states"...Read Station is not allowing the user to lighten or darken images at window level ..they can't mark images as dictated... " The problem resolution is documented as " ...took care of the issue." There is no additional information maintained for this complaint.

- A complaint received on January 19, 2010, for the PACS device states " ... a study would not burn on a cd for a patient... " The problem resolution is documented as " ...took care of the issue..." There is no additional information for this complaint.

FDA's Response to Observation 4 of 11 – Your response states your firm " ...has evaluated customer complaints but has not followed a formal procedure with documentation. We will establish and implement quality procedures to document and evaluate customer complaints....A complete written, reviewed, and approved set of procedures and process implementation will be completed by August 31, 2010...." We have reviewed your response, dated June 2, 2010, and have concluded it is inadequate because your firm did not demonstrate implementation for receiving, reviewing, and evaluating complaints for the PACS device by a designated unit within the firm.

Warning Letter Ten (September 2010)

Observation 3 of 6 – Failure to establish and maintain procedures for receiving, reviewing, and evaluating complaints and failure to maintain complaint files, as required by 21 CFR 820.198(a).

For example, you do not have a written complaint procedure nor do you maintain complaint files for the complaints stated to the FDA investigator that your firm received concerning the zIVF-AIRe™ 100C Photo-Catalytic Air Purifier.

FDA's Response to Observation 3 of 6 – We have reviewed your response and have concluded that it is inadequate. Your firm has not adequately addressed the requirements of 21 CFR 820.198(a) nor have you identified any systemic corrective actions regarding the lack of procedures for the receipt, review, and evaluation of complaints by a formally designated unit. Your firm has not provided a written complaint procedure nor have you provided complaint files for the complaints stated to the FDA investigator that you received concerning the zIVF-AIRe™ 100C Photo-Catalytic Air Purifier.

Quality System Regulation - 21 CFR, Part 820

QSR – Subpart M – Records

Section 820.180 General Requirements

All records required by this part shall be maintained at the manufacturing establishment or other location that is reasonably accessible to responsible officials of the manufacturer and to employees of FDA designated to perform inspections. Such records, including those not stored at the inspected establishment, shall be made readily available for review and copying by FDA employee(s). Such records shall be legible and shall be stored to minimize deterioration and to prevent loss. Those records stored in automated data processing systems shall be backed up.

(a)Confidentiality. Records deemed confidential by the manufacturer may be marked to aid FDA in determining whether information may be disclosed under the public information regulation in part 20 of this chapter.

(b)Record retention period. All records required by this part shall be retained for a period of time equivalent to the design and expected life of the device, but in no case less than 2 years from the date of release for commercial distribution by the manufacturer.

(c)Exceptions. This section does not apply to the reports required by 820.20(c) Management review, 820.22 Quality audits, and supplier audit reports used to meet the requirements of 820.50(a) Evaluation of suppliers, contractors, and consultants, but does apply to procedures established under these provisions. Upon request of a designated employee of FDA, an employee in management with executive responsibility shall certify in writing that the management reviews and quality audits required under this part, and supplier audits where applicable, have been performed and documented, the dates on which they were performed, and that any required corrective action has been undertaken.

Section 820.181 Device Master Record

Each manufacturer shall maintain device master records (DMR's). Each manufacturer shall ensure that each DMR is prepared and approved in accordance with 820.40. The DMR for each type of device shall include, or refer to the location of, the following information:

(a) Device specifications including appropriate drawings, composition, formulation, component specifications, and software specifications;

(b) Production process specifications including the appropriate equipment specifications, production methods, production procedures, and production environment specifications;

(c) Quality assurance procedures and specifications including acceptance criteria and

the quality assurance equipment to be used;

(d) Packaging and labeling specifications, including methods and processes used; and

(e) Installation, maintenance, and servicing procedures and methods.

Section 820.184 Device History Record

Each manufacturer shall maintain device history records (DHR's). Each manufacturer shall establish and maintain procedures to ensure that DHR's for each batch, lot, or unit are maintained to demonstrate that the device is manufactured in accordance with the DMR and the requirements of this part. The DHR shall include, or refer to the location of, the following information:

(a) The dates of manufacture;

(b) The quantity manufactured;

(c) The quantity released for distribution;

(d) The acceptance records which demonstrate the device is manufactured in accordance with the DMR;

(e) The primary identification label and labeling used for each production unit; and

(f) Any device identification(s) and control number(s) used.

Section 820.186 Quality System Record

Each manufacturer shall maintain a quality system record (QSR). The QSR shall include, or refer to the location of, procedures and the documentation of activities required by this part that are not specific to a particular type of device(s), including, but not limited to, the records required by 820.20. Each manufacturer shall ensure that the QSR is prepared and approved in accordance with 820.40 .

Section 820.198 Complaints

(a) Each manufacturer shall maintain complaint files. Each manufacturer shall establish and maintain procedures for receiving, reviewing, and evaluating complaints by a formally designated unit. Such procedures shall ensure that:

(1) All complaints are processed in a uniform and timely manner;

(2) Oral complaints are documented upon receipt; and

(3) Complaints are evaluated to determine whether the complaint represents an event which is required to be reported to FDA under part 803 of this chapter, Medical Device Reporting.

(b) Each manufacturer shall review and evaluate all complaints to determine whether an investigation is necessary. When no investigation is made, the manufacturer shall maintain a record that includes the reason no investigation was made and the name of the individual responsible for the decision not to investigate.

(c) Any complaint involving the possible failure of a device, labeling, or packaging to meet any of its specifications shall be reviewed, evaluated, and investigated, unless such investigation has already been performed for a similar complaint and another investigation is not necessary.

(d) Any complaint that represents an event which must be reported to FDA under part 803 of this chapter shall be promptly reviewed, evaluated, and investigated by a designated individual(s) and shall be maintained in a separate portion of the complaint files or otherwise clearly identified. In addition to the information required by 820.198(e), records of investigation under this paragraph shall include a determination of:

(1) Whether the device failed to meet specifications;

(2) Whether the device was being used for treatment or diagnosis; and

(3) The relationship, if any, of the device to the reported incident or adverse event.

(e) When an investigation is made under this section, a record of the investigation shall be maintained by the formally designated unit identified in paragraph (a) of this section. The record of investigation shall include:

(1) The name of the device;

(2) The date the complaint was received;

(3) Any device identification(s) and control number(s) used;

(4) The name, address, and phone number of the complainant;

(5) The nature and details of the complaint;

(6) The dates and results of the investigation;

(7) Any corrective action taken; and

(8) Any reply to the complainant.

(f) When the manufacturer's formally designated complaint unit is located at a site separate from the manufacturing establishment, the investigated complaint(s) and the record(s) of investigation shall be reasonably accessible to the manufacturing establishment.

(g) If a manufacturer's formally designated complaint unit is located outside of the United States, records required by this section shall be reasonably accessible in the United States at either:

(1) A location in the United States where the manufacturer's records are regularly kept; or

(2) The location of the initial distributor.

Records

Breaking down this requirement, the first salient point is that records **SHALL** be maintained at the device manufacturer or another accessible location. This does not mean an employee's garage. The records must be reasonably accessible and quickly retrievable when the agency shows up on the doorstep for a friendly visit. For example, storing records in Dr. D's garage would be a bad thing. With a third fridge for storing cold beer, pool supplies stored in a corner, and dog food for my big dogs ear the atrium door; not only does the ability to prevent damage to records come into play, the safety of individuals may come into question, especially if the dogs are in the garage. My recommendation is to define, by procedure, how long records are retained on site, and when records should be sent to the archives.

Additionally, ensure the record storage facility such as Iron Mountain (Dr. D is not a paid spokesperson for this supplier), is listed on the Approved Supplier List (ASL). Furthermore, ensure the supplier quality organization adds the record storage facility to the assessment list. Finally, I recommend putting the record retention facility through the proverbial paces. For example, if an FDA inspection is pending, notify the record retention facility in advance. I strongly recommend a few dry runs by requesting records and verifying the speed of delivery and accuracy.

Another significant concern, when dealing with record storage and retention, is the preservation of the actual records. If a device manufacturer really wants get on the good side of the FDA, request records from an offsite storage location; and present records that appear to have been a family meal for the local rodent population. Now you must be saying to yourselves, no way this could possibly happen Dr. D! Guess what, take it to the bank, it has happened, along with fire and water damaged records. Can you say Form 483? Finally, if a device manufacturer has automated systems, electronic media, and other electronic data devices; these types of records must also be backed up. It is up to the device manufacturer to decide the frequency and type of storage. However, the term "fire-proof" always comes to mind. The terms duplicate copy and stored off-site also come to mind.

Confidentiality

This requirement is pretty self-explanatory. If a device manufacturer provides the FDA with a record that contains proprietary information, the record (all pages) should be stamped with a confidentiality stamp. It is Dr. D's strong opinion, the stamp's font should be large, bold, contain the manufacturer's name, date released, with bright red ink employed. Otherwise, the Freedom of Information Act could result in proprietary information being released to the public. In this scenario, the public can be equated to the competition.

Record Retention Period

Reflecting back to warning letter depicted in this chapter, the minimum requirement is ***"2 years from the date of release for commercial distribution by the manufacturer."*** This is not a DG rule, but a QSR requirement that is cut and dry. One of the mistakes Dr. D sees device manufacturers make is retaining all records either forever or far too long. The doctor strongly suggests that device manufacturers develop a comprehensive record retention procedure that clearly delineates the retention period for every-single type of record. For example, and only a very small sample, purchase orders, calibration records, receiving inspection records, preventive maintenance records, bio-testing, environmental monitoring etc., should each have their very own retention time period. It is up to the device manufacturer to decide how long; however hint, hint, remember the minimum 2-year QSR requirement.

Exceptions

Dr. D hates exceptions to the rules, which is pretty funny coming from a guy that broke all of the rules as a young engineer. However, there are exceptions delineated under 820.180 of the QSR. Exceptions to section 820.180 are *"the reports required by 820.20(c) Management review, 820.22 Quality audits, and supplier audit reports used to meet the requirements of 820.50(a) Evaluation of suppliers, contractors, and consultants, but does apply to procedures established under these provisions."* However, device manufacturers still must provide evidence that these types of activities have occurred. This typically can be accomplished by providing a signed and dated attendance sheet and agenda as evidence the event occurred. Additionally, if these activities required corrective action, evidence of correction shall be provided to the FDA, upon request. Remember, CAPA is one area the agency will have a proverbial field day, if a device manufacturer is not proactive in their approach to pursuing effective corrective and preventive action.

Device Master Record

The salient concept associated with 820.181 is that DMR's be properly "prepared and approved." Additionally, there should be a DMR for every single device designed and manufactured, regardless of regulatory path, i.e., 510(k), PMA, etc. If the entire DMR process is found not to be in compliance with the QSR, device manufacturers, as a minimum, can expect a Form 483 when the agency shows up for a friendly visit. Worse case, a warning letter might make its way into the hands of the Chief Executive Officer (CEO) and Chief Jailable Officer (CJO), if enough compliance issues are identified during an inspection. Regardless, these regulatory actions can and will result in a significant interruption in the day-to-day activities of device manufacturers that violate the Code.

Device Specifications

As part of the DMR, device manufacturers are expected to retain specific types of records. For example, specifications applicable to the device, device drawings, component specifications, software specifications, production process and procedures, quality procedures, packaging specifications, labeling specifications, and procedures associated with maintenance and servicing need to be compiled into the DMR and retained. Remember the construction and long-term sustaining of the DMR is not optional. In fact, the DMR should be treated as a living and breathing document receptacle, as it will never remain in a static state.

Production Process Specifications

As part of the production-process specification requirement, it is not enough to retain only documented production processes. The agency is expecting to see significantly more granularity. For example, for production processes, equipment specifications, specific equipment settings, environmental conditions for production areas, applicable production methods, and test methods need to be captured in the DMR. Each of these documents should also be supported by evidence of verification and validation activities when appropriate. Production processes, procedures, environmental conditions, etc., are not worth a hill of beans if there is not technical data and rationale to substantiate accuracy and repeatability.

Quality Assurance Procedures

Similar to the production process requirements, applicable quality procedures, specifications, acceptance criteria, inspection equipment, shall be included into the DMR. Once again, significant granularity is expected in support of determining that quality assurance procedures and processes applied are effective. For example, if acceptance criterion involves employing specific types of measuring equipment, the effectiveness of the overall inspection process must be evaluated. If the criterion employed for determining product acceptance is not accurate and repeatable, a device manufacturer does not have a viable acceptance process, end of story.

Packaging and Labeling Specifications

Device manufacturers can take it to the proverbial bank, the possibility for the agency to identify finished devices as misbranded if the packaging and labeling does not match the specifications depicted within the DMR. Can you say RECALL? Yes, once again Dr. D has been able to invoke that nasty 6-letter word, sorry. The QSR requirement is to ensure manufacturers retain the actual and current product packaging and labeling specifications in the DMR. Additionally, when Dr. D states "current" the doctor means it. The doctor has experienced, first hand, when a device manufacturer does an admirable job of documenting the initial release of packaging and labeling specifications; however, fails to manage change. Packaging and labeling methodologies, content, specifications, etc. often do not remain in a static state. When specifications change, the DMR is the appropriate receptacle to capture these changes. Furthermore, methods, processes, and procedures employed as part of packaging and labeling shall also be retained in the DMR. For example, a **validated process** for pouch sealing or the actual affixing of the correct label on a device carton shall be included in the DMR.

Installation, Maintenance, and Servicing Procedures

The record retention for installation, maintenance, and servicing methods, processes, and procedures is also redundant to the previously discussed DMR requirements. Detailed procedures and methods shall be placed into the DMR and retained. Once again, if changes to the applicable procedures and methods occur, the changes, once reviewed and approved, need to be placed into the DMR. As the doctor stated earlier, the DMR is really a dynamic document receptacle (living and breathing file). In fact, the doctor has never seen a DMR remain in a steady state.

Device History Record

As with all elements of the QSR, the basic requirement will typically begin with the phrase; "*Each manufacturer shall establish and maintain procedures.*" Right out of the starting gate the FDA is clearly dictating that procedures are required, as in DG rule # 6, – All procedures, work instructions, drawings, specifications, etc. must be written, well-documented, and controlled within a defined document control system. Through the QSR, the DHR is linked backed to the DMR. For example, the DHR is the receptacle of document evidence that each manufactured device, batch, or lot of devices has been manufactured in accordance with the DMR. Additionally, the QSR provides sufficient granularity in regards to DHR content and the providing of pointers for specific pieces of information. As a minimum, the DHR shall include:

1. The actual date a device, batch, or lot was manufactured;

2. The actual quantity of devices manufactured;

3. The actual quantity of devices accepted and entered into distribution;

4. All of the records, inspection results, test results, evidence of sterilization, and other quality and manufacturing records that support devices being manufactured in accordance with the DMR;

5. A copy of the actual product label (pouch and carton) and the Directions for Use (DFU); and

6. Any additional identification, serial, or control numbers employed.

Remember, a good rule of thumb is to ensure all documentation relating to the actual manufacturing of a finished medical device shall be retained in the DHR. The DHR is the documented evidence needed, by device manufacturers, to support compliance to the QSR. Why? Because documented evidence is always a device manufacturer's best defense during an FDA inspection.

Quality System Record

The doctor's experience in industry leads him to opine that the creation of a well-written procedure is needed to achieve compliance to the QSR (both acronyms). For starters, all quality system procedures, associated documentation, and records, need to be legible. Dr. D always recommends implementing a strong program for Good Documentation Practices (GDP) supported by training, (don't you just love the acronyms). Additionally, if a device manufacturer chooses to employ a single procedure to drive compliance to the QSR, the procedure must be all-encompassing. What does that mean Dr. D? The doctor recommends creating a procedure that has three specific sections delineating; (a) the types of procedures, documentation, and records; (b) the storage location for procedures, documentation, and records; and (c) the actual planned retention timeframe for procedures, documentation, and records. In fact, Dr. D would label the major sections of this procedure as:

1. Types of Procedures, Documentation, and Records;

2. Storage Location of Procedures, Documentation, and Records; and

3. Planned Retention Time of Procedures, Documentation, and Records.

Additionally, if the QSR (acronym one) is managed electronically, the entire electronic process should be delineated within the procedure. Furthermore, when assigning retention timeframes, ensure the years specified are realistic. For example, Standard Operating Procedures (SOP) should be retained for the duration or as Dr. D would say, "a FOREVER Record!" Other quality system record-retention timeframes should be premised on importance. For example, Dr. D loves the number seven (7). That said, the doctor recommends retaining most quality-system records for at least 7-years. Remember the FDA has their own requirement for record retention; "*All records required by this part shall be retained for a period of time equivalent to the design and expected life of the device, but in no case less than 2 years from the date of release for commercial distribution by the manufacturer.*" Finally, regardless of the approach pursued for meeting the QSR (both acronyms); "*Each manufacturer shall ensure that the QSR is prepared and approved in accordance with 820.40.*"

Complaints

Complaint, complaints, and more complaints, if you want to play in the medical-device industry sandbox, device manufacturers better get accustomed to the concept. Complaint and complaint handling is a daily part of life for medical device companies. Customer complaints run the complaint gamut, with some being as simple as the ink smeared on a device-package label or problematic such as a sterile-barrier breach. Complaints can also be categorized as major or significant when a device problem results in patient injury or death (a.k.a. adverse events). As many of you already know, complaints also drive input into the FDA's Manufacturer and User Facility Device Experience (MAUDE) Database, as adverse events are required to be reported employing FDA Form 3500(a). Device manufacturers should have robust procedures that define their specific program requirements in regards to post-market surveillance activities. Regardless, complaints require a significant organizational commitment to ensure a fastidious and consistent approach to complaint management is sustained. Because the complaint requirements delineated within the QSR contain a significant amount of granularity, this chapter contains guidance for complying with 820.198, subsections a, b, and c. All of the requirements device manufacturers are mandated by law to comply with can appear as a farraginous (look-it-up if you must) assortment of regulations, mandates, and statutory requirements; however, remember this, Dr. D will never steer the readers in the wrong direction.

So let Dr. D begin with another broken-record time, what part of not having effective written procedures and adhering to written procedures do device manufacturers still not understand? As with all of the requirements delineated within the QSR, the establishment and management of complaint files requires written procedures. Additionally, because the management of complaints is really a unique process, the FDA expects device manufacturers to establish a dedicated functional group for managing complaints. Furthermore, the agency's expectation is that all types of complaints; (a) formal (e.g., from a physician or patient); (b) oral (e.g., a simple phone call); (c) complaints identified in a magazine, paper, or periodical, a.k.a. literature review; or (d) complaints coming from a third party (e.g. family or friend) find their way into the complaint management system. Finally, Dr. D strongly recommends opening a complaint file for each complaint received. It is much easier to manage and track complaints when this approach is pursued.

Procedure Elements

As a starting point, the QSR requires three salient components for inclusion into the complaint management system. The first element of the complaint system should address the manner in which all complaints will be managed. For example, the procedure should contain specific references, such as:

1. Time required for processing complaints, including closure;

2. The time required for the actual complaint investigation;

3. Specific elements addressing the investigational process when product is not returned for evaluation; and

4. In general the overall handling, or as the QSR states, "uniform" handling of complaints.

As depicted in the previous paragraph, the complaint procedure must clearly delineate the process in which "ALL COMPLAINTS" are entered into the complaint management system. The procedure must be robust enough to ensure complaints that represent an adverse event (serious patient injury or death) make their way into the MAUDE database in accordance with 21 CFR, Part 803. If the conclusion reached, as part of the complaint investigation process, points to an adverse event, an MDR is required. It is Dr. D's professional opinion, it is always better for device manufacturers to pursue a conservative approach when reporting MDRs. "Confucius say it is always better to over-report and stay in the good graces of the FDA then to under report and receive warning letter," just kidding on the Confucius part.

Complaint Investigation

As many of you already know, Dr. D strongly believes compliance to the QSR does not entail rocket science. That said, here is another rocket science moment, the FDA actually expects device manufacturers to investigate the complaints they receive. Additionally, device manufacturers are required to keep accurate records of the complaint investigations pursued. If a decision is made not to open or pursue an investigation, that decision still needs to be captured and retained. Why? Because documented evidence of compliance is always a device manufacturer's best defense during one of the friendly visits from the FDA. Furthermore, if a decision is made not to investigate, the QSR demands that the decision maker's name be documented as part of the decision process. Can you say Chief Jailable Officer (CJO)? It is Dr. D's recommendation that some level of review occur for each complaint. The information gleaned from this exercise will be extremely useful when it comes time to execute complaint trending and documenting the root-causes of complaints. Besides, without an effective complaint investigation process, how can device manufacturers ever be expected to fix potential problems associated with device safety and efficacy?

Complaints Associated with Device Failure, Labeling, or Packaging

If a received complaint is directly related to a device failure, accuracy of the labeling, or concerns over device packaging (e.g., sterile barrier breach), the device manufacturer better be prepared to pursue a robust investigation. In short, if the device, device labeling, or device packaging, fails to meet the documented and approved product specification pursuing an investigation is in order. Now granted, 820.198 - subsection (c) allows device manufacturers some latitude in regards to previously documented complaints; however, a pointer must be clearly made back to these previously analyzed complaints. If the agency feels that there are far too many incidents pointing back to previously analyzed complaints, and these complaints are directly related to adverse events, the device manufacturer should probably begin preparations for a "for-cause" or should I say, "Directed" visit from the agency. If the complaints being received point to the device in question injuring patients, be prepared to execute that six-letter word "RECALL." There goes the doctor invoking that nasty word again. When creating a procedure for complaint management, Dr. D always prefers the use of flow charts and decision trees. With the help of engineers, clinicians, quality, regulatory and other functional organizations, that exude some influence over complaint handling and management, effective decision trees, with escalation clauses, e.g., file or not file an MDR, can be created.

Complaint Elevation

Section 820,198 (d) delineates the requirement that reportable complaints, to the FDA, "shall be promptly reviewed, evaluated, and investigated." The expectation is that these investigations are prioritized and expedited. Taking 3-months to report a reportable event is just not going to work. In fact, according to 21 CFR, Part 803 the requirement for adverse-event reporting is 30-days for manufacturers and 10-days for device users, unless it has been determined that the device poses an "unreasonable risk of substantial harm to the public health," then the timeline is accelerated to 5-days. Based on the warning letters depicted above, device manufacturers that fail to adhere to the QSR requirements for managing complaints, will receive a warning letter. Dr. D guarantees it.

Additionally, 820,198 (d) requires a designated individual(s) to promptly review, evaluate, and investigate all complaints. The doctor strongly suggests that the individual(s) performing this review is/are competent and capable of making fundamentally sound decisions, premised on the outcome of each complaint investigation. Furthermore, the results of each review, evaluation, and subsequent investigation need to be collected and placed into a complaint file. The doctor strongly recommends opening a separate complaint file for each complaint received. Finally, the complaint records, in addition to what will be covered in the next section, shall contain:

1. A determination as to whether or not the device failed to meet specification (a.k.a. the product specification);

2. Whether the device was employed for a therapeutic or diagnostic application; and

3. The link between the device and the reported complaint (incident) and subsequent adverse event.

Complaint Investigation Records

In addition to the three (3) items discussed in the previous section, the FDA has additional requirements, delineated within the QSR, for basic complaint data. One salient point to remember is the link between complaints and the Corrective and Preventive Action System (CAPA). In many instances, the outcome of a complaint investigation will drive the need for CAPA to remediate a device performance issue, e.g., failure for a coronary stent to deploy. As part of the agency's approach to inspections, the Quality

System Inspection Technique (QSIT) will focus on complaints and CAPA as potential entry points into a device manufacturer's quality system.

So what additional information should the complaint record contain? Not wanting to state the obvious, the complaint record should contain all information relevant to the complaint investigation. Additionally, the QSR requires:

1. The actual name of the device, e.g. Acme Super Catheter;

2. The date the complaint was actually received, reported, or the device manufacturer actually became aware;

3. Identifiers specific to the device, e.g., batch and control numbers;

4. The name, address, and telephone number of the individual and/or organization reporting the complaint;

5. The nature of the complaint augmented by obtaining as much detailed information as possible (hopefully something more than the device is broken);

6. The dates associated with the investigation and the results of the investigation (make sure the name of the investigator(s) is/are also captured);

7. Identification of the need to elevate the results of the investigation into the CAPA system (including CAPA number); and

8. A copy of the reply letter back to the person and/or organization making the complaint (Dr. D recommends sending the letters with proof of delivery required – Fed-X, UPS, etc.).

Dr. D also recommends ensuring decision making in regards to MDR reporting also be included in the complaint record. An additional watch out, complaint data and complaint trending should be included in management review. Finally, the entire complaint management process should have a specified timeline as to how long complaint investigations take. If the device manufacturer puts into writing (a.k.a., a procedure) that the entire process will take 12-months, rest-assured, the FDA will take exception to the length of time specified. Considering the amount of time it may take to: (a) return a device back to the manufacturer; (b) complete a detailed investigation; (c) summarize the data in a written report; (d) open up a CAPA (if deemed appropriate); and (e) send a reply back to the complainant; Dr. D strongly opines the entire process should not exceed 60-days. However, most device manufacturers' lean toward 90-days as policy; and Dr. D fundamentally disagrees with 90-days.

Complaint Management Unit Located at a Site Separate from Manufacturing

The requirements for managing a complaint-handling unit, which is detached from the actual manufacturing facility, are pretty basic. For starters, yes a written procedure is a salient requirement. However, the actual dynamics of complaint management will differ versus a self-contained business unit. The regulation, 820.198(f), requires two fundamental objectives be attained. Number one, the results of all **complaint investigations** should be readily accessible by the manufacturing facility. Number two – the **complaint records** should be readily accessible by the manufacturing facility. This task is relatively easy to achieve and can be accomplished by employing a single complaint receptacle for the entire organization. This can be broken down even further into specific business units. There are several electronic complaint- management systems available (Part 11 compliant), which can be employed as a solution for complaint management for organizations both large and small. Additionally, pursing an electronic system approach, for complaint management, allows device manufacturers to trend and report results as part of the management-review process. Remember, complaints must be included as an input to management review. Besides, Dr. D strongly believes that information gleaned from customer complaints should be used to drive continuous-improvement practices that improve the safety and efficacy of devices.

Complaint Management Unit Located Outside of the United States (OUS)

Similar to complaint management and processing being performed at a location other than the actual manufacturing facility, a complaint management unit maintained OUS is an acceptable practice, providing a robust-written procedure delineating the complaint-management process exists. Once again, records of each complaint must be "reasonably accessible" within the United States. Therefore, if a device manufacturer's complaint management center is located in Katmandu (being managed by Bob Seeger – just kidding), the device manufacturer needs to ensure complaint records are accessible at either: (1) a location identified within the states, where records are routinely stored; or (2) the location of the distributor that sold the medical devices (if applicable and linked to the actual complaint and/or adverse event). Basically, each device manufacturer must take control of their destiny in regards to complaints. Remember, it is not enough to have successfully opened, analyzed, investigated, compiled, and stored complaint records. Subsections (f) and (g), of 820.198, specifically requires complaint records to be accessible. In fact, the accessibility piece will become an important feature, not if but when the FDA decides to pay a device manufacturer a friendly visit. Trust Dr. D when I say, "If device complaints are being reported as adverse events; and the number of events are perceived to be excessive, expect a visit from the agency." When your Chief Jailable Officer (CJO) is sitting across from the investigator, he or she will have a newfound appreciation for having complete, accurate, and accessible complaint records for the agency to review. Why? Because documented evidence of compliance with the QSR is always a device manufacturer's best defense during an inspection. Otherwise, can you say, "Where do I sign the Form 483?" Finally, if a device manufacturer cannot convince the agency that the complaint management system is effective; and that the adverse events are directly related to product safety and efficacy, be prepared for that ugly 6-letter word "Recall," Yes – Dr. D has once again mentioned that cursed word.

Takeaways from Chapter 18

Remember, accurate records and documentation is always a device manufacturer's best friend during FDA inspections. Dr. D strongly suggests that the record retention procedure be extremely prescriptive in regards to how long each type of record is retained and actual storage locations. Please do not forget to add suppliers selected for off-site record storage to the ASL; and ensure that these record storage facilities are audited. Just because management reviews are not explicitly covered under this section of the QSR, does not mean records associated with this activity should not be retained. This type of record is equally important.

Ensuring the DMR is the receptacle for the appropriate type of records and the ongoing sustaining of the DMR are the basic salient requirements associated with 820.181. Remember, the DMR will never remain in a steady state. As products mature, manufacturing technology changes, or when product complaints occur, device manufactures are driven to modify applied methodologies, processes, and procedures.

When changes occur, these changes shall be captured in the DMR. Fail to adequately manage the DMR process, and device manufacturers will be duly rewarded by their good friends at the agency.

The DHR contains a number of records that support a device manufacturer's claim that a medical device was manufactured in accordance with the DMR. A DHR, which is organized and contains complete and accurate information, is a fundamental requirement needed to support claims of compliance to the QSR during a friendly visit by the FDA. A complete and accurate DHR will be a valuable asset should devices need to be recovered due to a RECALL.

The key for compiling a QSR and ongoing compliance with the QSR (yes – two acronyms), is the establishment of a well-written procedure. The agency really wants device manufacturers to have quick access to procedures, documentation, and records compiled as part of a QSR. Dr. D cannot think of a more efficient approach than creating a procedure, with tables, that (a) accurately identify the type of procedure, documentation, or record; (b) accurately identify the location the procedure, documentation, or record is being stored; and (c) the actual retention period for each procedure, documentation, or record.

Since the procedural requirement continues to be the most salient requirement associated with compliance with the QSR, there are five additional takeaways associated with the procedural requirement.

1. Device manufacturers must ensure complaints from all potential sources are collected and entered into their complaint management system.

2. Each complaint needs to be reviewed and a documented decision made in

regards to pursue or not pursue an investigation.

3. Where investigational results point to the conclusion that an adverse event has occurred, the device manufacturer must file an MDR.

4. Dr. D recommends a complaint file be opened for each complaint received.

5. Confucius says, "It is better to over report than under report MDRs."

Complaints "shall be promptly reviewed, evaluated, and investigated. Documenting the results is a given, maintaining accurate records is a given, reporting adverse events is a given, correcting problems is a given, and having a WRITTEN PROCEDURE is a given. However, failure to manage complaints in accordance with 820.198 is not a given; and can be equated to giving the agency an open invitation to show up on your doorstep with a Form 482 in hand.

Finally; (a) complaints can be managed by a separate organization located in a facility detached from manufacturing operations; and (b) complaints can be managed OUS. The salient point, when managing complaint externally, is the accessibility of complaint records, regardless of their location. This information needs to be accessible. The information collected as part of the overall complaint process will drive the decision-making process in regards to reporting adverse events; and the resolution of device issues through corrective and preventive action.

Chapter 19 – Servicing

21 CFR, Part 820

Subpart N

Section 820.200

Chapter Nineteen – Servicing

Servicing is a functional requirement, mandated by the Quality System Regulation (QSR), and often overlooked by device manufacturers. Granted, 21 CFR, Part 820.200 is often associated with capital equipment; however, the manufacturers of disposable medical devices still must consider the requirement. As with all aspects of the QSR, a written procedure is required, delineating a device manufacturer's steps for compliance with the requirement. If servicing is not relevant for the device manufacturer, written rationale as to why servicing is not a requirement should still be generated. As many of you already know, Dr. D is always preaching to the choir in regards to compliance. The doctor, being a precentor (look-it up) of compliance to regulations for the medical device industry, strongly believes in the need for well-written procedures and written rationales to support ongoing compliance to the QSR and other mandated regulatory requirements, required to participate in the device industry. Written procedures supporting compliance to the mandated industry regulations should be considered the price of admission.

Warning Letter Violations

Dr. D spent a significant amount of time searching the FDA's warning-letter database in search of enforcement actions depicting compliance issues due to servicing. I was able to locate two violators of the QSR, with each being duly rewarded with a warning letter. Each of the violators had one common problem, failure to establish and maintain procedures. Device manufacturers need to remember that it is an ineluctable (look-it up if you must) fact that you will receive Form 483s and potentially warning letters for not establishing procedures. As Dr. D has often stated, compliance to DG Rule # 6 is not an option; "All procedures, work instructions, drawings, specifications, etc.

must be written, well-documented, and controlled within a defined document control system."

The second warning-letter recipient clearly endeared their organization with the agency, as evidenced by two (2) of their ten (10) observations, noted in the warning letter, rooted in servicing issues. Not only did this device manufacturer fail to establish procedures for servicing, the servicing reports being collected from the field were not being appropriately analyzed employing statistical techniques. Although the doctor has not leaped onto his soapbox too much in regards to the importance of analyzing collected data, what is the point of data collection if the results are not analyzed, trended, and if necessary, do not drive change?

Warning Letter One (June 2010)

> *Observation 5 of 6* – Failure to establish Servicing procedures as required by 21 CFR 820.00(a). Specially, your service manual does not address issues related to software failures.

Warning Letter Two (May 2009)

> *Observation 7 of 10* – Failure to establish and maintain instructions and procedures for performing and verifying that the servicing meets specified requirements, as required by 21 CFR 820.200(a). Specifically, your firm does not have any procedures for servicing.

> *Observation 8 of 10* – Failure to analyze service reports with appropriate statistical methodology, as required by 21 CFR 820.200(b). Specifically, your firm does, not have any procedures for analyzing service reports. In addition, the service reports were not analyzed following appropriate statistical methods.

Quality System Regulation - 21 CFR, Part 820

QSR – Subpart N – Servicing

Section 820.200 Servicing

> *(a) Where servicing is a specified requirement, each manufacturer shall establish and*

maintain instructions and procedures for performing and verifying that the servicing meets the specified requirements.

(b) Each manufacturer shall analyze service reports with appropriate statistical methodology in accordance with 820.100.

(c) Each manufacturer who receives a service report that represents an event which must be reported to FDA under part 803 of this chapter shall automatically consider the report a complaint and shall process it in accordance with the requirements of 820.198.

(d) Service reports shall be documented and shall include:
  (1) The name of the device serviced;
  (2) Any device identification(s) and control number(s) used;
  (3) The date of service;
  (4) The individual(s) servicing the device;
  (5) The service performed; and
  (6) The test and inspection data.

Servicing

Not wanting to state the obvious but obliged to do so, section 820.200 is divided into four subsections (a through d). In the eyes of the FDA, there is sufficient granularity delineated within the servicing section for device manufacturers to develop a procedure, or if necessary, a set of procedures, incorporating servicing into their quality model. Remember, depending on the nature of the device being distributed into the US markets, a full-blown procedure may not be required; however, device manufacturers are compelled to at least develop a procedure and written rationale as to why the servicing requirement is not relevant to their business model. Dr. D strongly believes that there are no such animals as minimum-level of compliance or maximum-level of compliance. There is only compliance, period!

Establish and Maintain Instructions & Procedures

The first section of the servicing requirement defines the necessity for device manufacturers to establish servicing, with the caveat that states, "Where servicing is a specific requirement." As Dr. D stated in the previous section establishing procedures is a salient requirement. Even though the agency has given device manufacturers the proverbial "get-out-of-jail free card" a written - albeit brief procedure, is strongly recommended for device manufacturers that claim servicing is not specific requirement. One of Dr. D's favorite mantras is and will continue to be; "documented evidence of compliance is a device manufacturer's best defense during an FDA inspection."

Analyze Service Reports

The second salient requirement of the servicing regulation is the actual analysis of the service reports employing recognized statistical methodologies. The bottom-line requirement for service reports is extremely elementary. The reports contain data; and data screams to be analyzed. Besides, who wants to sit across from your friendly FDA investigator and attempt to explain that your organization collected data just for the sake of having data? What would be the point? Exactly, there would be no point, so just be prepared to ask, where do I sign the Form 483.

Event Reporting

The third salient requirement of the servicing regulation is that, if during the review of a service report it has been determined an adverse event has occurred (serious patient injury or death) the servicing record needs to be captured and recorded as a complaint that is reportable. Complaints shall be managed in accordance with 820.198. If you need a refresher on complaint management requirements, Dr. D would like to suggest rereading the previous chapter of this book, which delineated the requirements of an effective complaint-management system. Additionally, servicing records logged as complaints, and where the adverse events are deemed reportable, the events shall be reported to the agency in accordance with 21 CFR, Part 803. The form employed for reporting adverse events, Form 3500(a) can be downloaded from the www.fda.gov website. Furthermore, electronic reporting is now the preferred methodology of the agency.

Service Reports

Similar to other record requirements associated with the QSR, there are specific deliverables associated with service reports. The QSR mandates that at least six (6) pieces of information be collected and retained as part of ongoing compliance with the servicing requirements. These salient pieces of information are:

1. The actual name of the device that was serviced (preferably the registered legal name);

2. Device identification and control number (e.g., unit serial number);

3. The date the service was actually performed (self-explanatory – the doctor hopes);

4. The name of the individual performing the service (recommend capturing the name of the individual's organization if it is different from the manufacturer);

5. The nature of the service performed (self-explanatory); and

6. The actual inspection and/or test reports associated with the service (evidence that the service occurred and the piece of equipment is functioning within specification).

Although not specifically delineated within the regulation, Dr. D recommends capturing additional information ; (a) location of the unit being serviced; (b) reason behind the service call; (c) point of contact; (d) list of components replaced; (e) revision of software loaded; (f) operating hours, if captured by a meter on the piece of equipment being serviced; and (g) if the servicing was being performed during a full or blue moon (just kidding about the moon). These additional pieces of information, specifically information that modifies the as-built or as-shipped configuration should find its way back to the Device History Record (DHR). Additionally, if servicing is being performed to incorporate specific design changes, these should be captured in the Design History File (DHF). Furthermore, make sure these changes have been validated, and received the appropriate level of regulatory review and approval, including the FDA, if deemed appropriate.

Takeaways from Chapter 19

One of the reason the QSR has a servicing requirement, other than the obvious patient and user safety and efficacy, is to protect end users from the infamous red-light guarantee, a.k.a., as long as you see the red-tail lights of the shipping truck, the equipment is guaranteed to function. All kidding aside, it really is a mission critical assignment to provide adequate servicing for equipment deployed in healthcare facilities, while ensuring all of the relevant servicing activities are recorded, tracked trended, analyzed, etc. Additionally, keeping track of changes to configuration becomes a daunting task if record keeping is poor. Dr. D has first-hand experience in executing recalls, damn there is that dirty 6-letter word again, because inadequate servicing records placed into question the actual configuration of equipment released into distribution. The root of the recall was nestled in record accuracy and ineffective management of service records. That said, unlike tossing a hand grenade, or the cliché "close but no cigars" record accuracy counts.

Chapter 20 – Statistical Techniques

21 CFR, Part 820

Subpart O

Section 820.250

Chapter Twenty – Statistical Techniques

In an adventure that began in early 2010, the doctor has been traversing through the Quality System Regulation (QSR), providing banausic (look-it up) insights and salient points for compliance, while injecting humor and some sarcasm from the perspective of a long-time quality professional. Dr. D's writing is motivated by the need to ensure all device manufacturers enjoy the success that can be eventuated from sustained compliance to the QSR. That said, 21 CFR, Part 820 – Subpart O (Statistical Techniques) is the proverbial "final act" in regards to the QSR.

Warning Letter Violations

Sometimes the doctor just feels like screaming – **AHHHHHHHHHHH!** For this chapter, the three lucky recipients of the FDA's "You Suck Award" (a.k.a. warning letter) each received an observation that commences with the infamous and often used introduction of "*Failure to Establish & Maintain Procedures.*" Week after week, the agency routinely inspects the effectiveness of device manufacturer's quality systems; and week after week, the FDA routinely issues Form 483s that often translate into warning letters. Dr. D sincerely hopes that the readers will take away from this chapter and all of the previous chapters of the book; procedures are everything in the medical device industry. The expectation of the FDA is that the procedures device manufacturers create encompass the entire QSR and not just the ones the device manufacturers believe they need to comply. People, I have been there and want to reinforce the belief that "**Warning Letters are no Fun!**"

For device manufacturer's wishing to exacerbate their predicament with the agency, go ahead and provide a response to an observation without sufficient evidence supporting the issues associated with an observation have been resolved. If there are

doubts about what the agency is looking for in regards to corrective action and closure,

pick up the phone and ask the agency for clarification, just do not shoot from the hip.

Two of the FDA's "You Suck Award" recipients provided the FDA with responses that

were deemed insufficient. Do you know what happens to device manufacturers that

provide poorly positioned responses to Form 483s? The Form 483s morph into warning

letters. Do you know what happens to device manufacturers that provide poorly

positioned responses to warning letters or fail to respond to a warning letter within 15-

days of receipt? They enter the FDA's house of pain and take the first giant leap toward

Consent Decree!

Warning Letter One (June 2010)

> *Observation 8 of 14* – Failure to establish and maintain adequate procedures to ensure that sampling methods are adequate for their intended use and to ensure that when changes occur the sampling plans are reviewed as required by 21 CFR 820.250(b). For example, your firm's procedure **(b)(4)** Sampling of Finished Products, Revision **(b)(4)** describes the requirements for collecting samples of the finished product. However, the procedure does not discuss sampling for additional testing to overcome a failure of the finished product, other than to say that an investigation shall be conducted. As a result, the **(b)(4)** which is integrity testing, was used to release lots of prefilled syringes when defects affecting the container closure integrity were found after or during manufacturing. Sampling for **(b)(4)** consisted of **(b)(4)** regardless of the size of the prefilled syringe lot. In some cases this size was as low as **(b)(4)** of the lot. Your firm released the following lots of I.V. Flush Syringes on the basis of **(b)(4)** per your firm's, **(b)(4)**
>
> a. **(b)(4)**
> b. **(b)(4)**
> c. **(b)(4)**

Warning Letter Two (May 2010)

> *Observation 6 of 6* – Failure to establish and maintain procedures for identifying valid statistical techniques required for establishing, controlling, and verifying the acceptability of process capabilities and product characteristics, as required by 21 CFR 820.250(a).

For example, there was no recognized sampling plan methodology incorporating a valid statistical technique to verify the acceptability of the process and take appropriate action when nonconforming components or products are identified that do not meet the acceptable quality limit (AQL).

FDA Response to Observation 6 of 6 – We have reviewed your response dated December 17, 2009, and have concluded that it is inadequate because it does not include documentation demonstrating that the sampling plan methodology issues have been appropriately addressed.

Warning Letter Three (March 2010)

Observation 5 of 5 – Failure to establish and maintain procedures for identifying valid statistical techniques required for establishing, controlling and verifying the acceptability of process capability and product characteristics, as required by 21 CFR § 820.250(a).

For example, your firm does not have adequate statistical rationale to support the techniques used in trending of customer complaints per your film's procedure SP-14122, "Complaint Trending and Escalation Process," revision F, issued October 02, 2008

FDA Response to Observation 5 of 5 – Your firm's response dated October 16, 2009, is not adequate because your firm has not provided adequate statistical rationale for your film's Complaint Trending and Escalation Process procedure. Please contact the Center for Devices and Radiological Health's (CDRH) Office of Compliance (OC) with further responses.

Quality System Regulation - 21 CFR, Part 820

QSR – Subpart O – Statistical Techniques

Section 820.250 Statistical Techniques

> *(a) Where appropriate, each manufacturer shall establish and maintain procedures for identifying valid statistical techniques required for establishing, controlling, and verifying the acceptability of process capability and product characteristics.*

> *(b) Sampling plans, when used, shall be written and based on a valid statistical rationale. Each manufacturer shall establish and maintain procedures to ensure that sampling methods are adequate for their intended use and to ensure that when changes occur the sampling plans are reviewed. These activities shall be documented.*

Statistical Techniques

Before I dive into statistical techniques, Dr. D would like to refresh the readers with a definition of statistics. According to Merriam-Webster's On-Line Dictionary, "*statistics*" is a branch of mathematics dealing with the collection, analysis, interpretation, and presentation of masses of numerical data. The doctor believes that device manufacturers need to understand the purpose and value of applied statistics in supporting decisions associated with initial design, process development, and ongoing compliance to a published and approved product specification. When Dr. D has the occasion to visit suppliers, and I ask about applied statistical methodologies, answering the doctor's question with, "we 100% inspect all characteristics," I must inform the suppliers this is not an acceptable statistical technique. In fact, it is not even an effective approach to inspection. My belief is that process capability studies, with the results interpreted in CpK and PpK, is the only true path to establishing effective statistical techniques and the rationale required by the regulation. When discussing the employment of statistical methodologies, Dr. D always like to point engineers in the direction of Juran's Quality Handbook, which some of us in the industry refer to as the Quality Engineer's Bible. Dr. D also recommends visiting Dr. Wayne Taylor's website and reading his work on effective sampling plans. Finally, with so many statistical tools available, such as Minitab™ (no – Dr. D is not a paid spokesperson for Minitab) there should never be an excuse for device manufacturers not having a robust and documented approach to statistical techniques..

Procedure(s)

It is now time for another Dr. D broken-record time. As the doctor has opined on multiple occasions; DG Rule # 6 is not an option; "All procedures, work instructions, drawings, specifications, etc. must be written, well-documented, and controlled within a defined document control system." Nestled into every single requirement of the QSR is the phase, "***Shall establish and maintain procedures.***" The text seems pretty clear to Dr. D, so I struggle to understand why device manufacturers continue to misinterpret the need for procedures. In regards to statistical techniques, the agency is really looking for device manufacturers to collect data and then interpret the results of the data through the application of statistics. For example, if Acme Device Corporation (fictional name) has a critical requirement for device length, the agency expects Acme to prove that the device meets this critical requirement on continuous basis. Can you say process capability studies? In this example, Acme should be collecting dimensional data and using statistics, e.g., to ascertain if ongoing processes are capable and remain in statistical process control – English translation "the device length is within specification and we have the data to prove it – done!" If Acme validated the process as being Six Sigma capable and the data is now trending below a PpK of 1.0, there now appears to be a problem. How a device manufacturer identifies the problem, though the employment of statistics, and how the problem is corrected is one of the fundamental foundations of this requirement. If device manufacturers are collecting data just for the sake of having the data, well – what is the point? In summarizing 820.250(a), device manufacturers shall have a procedure that delineates robust statistical methodologies for driving process control; and supporting ongoing inspection activities in determining that measured characteristics are acceptable and within their specification limits.

Sampling Plans

As I stated earlier, Dr. D strongly suggest reading Dr. Taylor's work on statistics and sampling plans as a whole. Additionally, the American Society for Quality maintains two of the most recognizable standards for determining appropriate sample sizes and creating effective sample plans, ANSI/ASQ Z1.4-2003 for the inspection of attributes and ANSI/ASQ Z1.9-2008 for the inspection of variables. Adherence to these mainstays of acceptable approaches to sampling methods will result in a solid foundation for device manufacturers to support compliance to 820.250. Over the years, I cannot count the times that Dr. D has been asked to evaluate the statistical significance, of legacy data, when the sample size employed was a N=3 or an N=5. Do you have any idea how difficult it is to defend that type of sample rationale to any regulatory body, especially the FDA? It is the doctor's opinion; there is no way to defend the approach, if it is documented by procedure. The approach is irresponsible, reprehensible, lackadaisical, nonsensical, impractical, laughable, and indefensible, when sitting across from the agency during one of their friendly visits.

To summarize, the doctor strongly suggests that the documented approach to sampling be premised on recognized standards. Not only does the sampling methodology need to be delineated with the procedure, so does the ability to adjust sampling plans premised on the results. The doctor strongly suggests that sampling plans are routinely reviewed and the results of the review documented. Additionally, the need to review sampling plans needs to be depicted in the actual procedure. Furthermore, sampling plans need to be linked back to risk and risk indices. When determining an appropriate level of sampling for a component or device, it is imperative that the PFMEA and DFMEA be evaluated. Why? Because the failure mode effects analysis (FMEA) will lead you to applying the appropriate sample size premised on the actual risk of failure. Finally, ensure your supplier base is capable of understanding and employing industry recognized statistical concepts. Suppliers that routinely employ effective statistical approaches to process control will be in position to deliver product that meet specification.

Takeaways from Chapter 20

There is a plethora of data, standards, and websites that can provide useful information needed to create robust procedure(s) for establishing effective statistical control. Additionally, this same information is available for establishing effective sampling plans. As captured in the warning letter extractions, the FDA will evaluate a device manufacturer's approach to statistics and sampling during one of their friendly visits. Establishing robust procedures, in advance, will mitigate the potential receipt of a Form 483.

Chapter 21 – Responding to an FDA Form 483

So the FDA has just completed a friendly visit to your facility; and the inspector has decided that your organization has deviated in regards to compliance with 21 CFR, Part 820, the Quality System Regulation (QSR) or another Part of the Code, e.g. 801, 803, etc., so now what? For starters, management can commence with the public floggings of all of the individuals responsible for the functional areas failing to pass muster during the inspection. Prior to signing the Form 483, the management representative can argue vehemently with the inspector, informing the individual that their observations are inaccurate, and thus alienating the agency. Another approach might be to climb onto the top of the table in the conference room and throw a tantrum, not unlike a spoiled two-year old. Even better, fake an immediate illness, let out a plangent scream of pain, run for the door, and never return. Besides, if the organization was laced with rabid readers of Dr. D's chrestomathies (look-it up), just maybe signing the old Form 483 might not have been necessary. Regardless, in this chapter, the doctor will focus on responding to Form 483 observations. Enjoy!

Sign the Blasted Form 483

During the final debrief by the inspector, when the observations are presented, ensure the organization fully understands the nature of each observation. If the observation is inaccurate and documented evidence exists, now would be a good time to ensure clarification of the issue, with the investigator, occurs. I recommend locking the door, and not letting the FDA depart the premises, until the observation is fully understood. Just do not attempt a kidnapping – just kidding. Dr. D has seen instances were an observation has been rescinded during the final debrief, when the correct or additional evidence or clarification is presented. If the observation has already been corrected, please provide the necessary evidence to the inspector. What one should never do is enter a protracted argument over observations. Once points have been made, and the basis of the observations understood, the Form 483 should be signed. Ensure the inspector fully understands that your organization is committed to correcting the deficiencies.

What is a Form 483 (Notice of Inspectional Observations)?

Section 704 of the Federal Food, Drug, and Cosmetic Act establishes the FDA's authority to inspect facilities that fall under the governance of the Act. Additionally, Section 704 requires the FDA to provide facilities inspected with a report that delineates all deviations noted during the inspection. From a historical perspective, the official birth year of the Form 483 was 1953, with the addition of Section 704(b) of the Act. The good news is that a formal response to the agency is not mandated by law. The bad news is that failure to respond to a Form 483 will in all likelihood result in the FDA's issuance of a warning letter against the organization failing to respond. Furthermore, there is a stated requirement that the initial response to the agency be made within 15-days (working days). That said, Dr. D **"STRONGLY RECOMMENDS"** all device manufacturers respond to each Form 483 observation within 15-days, even if you do not agree with the observation. In fact, now would be the time to formulate and finalize a salient position as to why your organization disagrees with an observation. At the end of the day, if the observation is minor, Dr. D always recommends just fixing the issue instead of arguing the relevancy with the agency. Why? Because the lost sleep, worrying about insignificant issues is just not worth the trouble.

Crafting a Response to the Form 483

First, begin by understanding why your organization received the Form 483. In the eyes of the agency, they issue Form 483s when an inspector determines an organization has failed to comply with a specific part of the code delineated under the Act. The FDA employs the Form 483 as a vehicle to ensure organizations quickly and properly correct all noted observations. Remember, a response is not mandated by law; however, the agency has the ability to unleash a whole lot of pain for organizations that chose not to comply with the request for correction. Trust Dr. D when I emphatically state, "If the agency is not happy with your organization's approach to responding to a Form 483, your organization is not going to be happy when they receive the warning letter." Simply stated, "Warning letters equate to pain!"

The next step is to ensure a response is drafted and returned to the agency within 15-working days. From the FDA's perspective, a prompt, and well-positioned response, equates to an organization taking the Form 483 seriously. Dr. D recommends always placing each observation into the Corrective and Preventive Action (CAPA) System, regardless of how innocuous an observation might be. This way progress for each of the observations can be tracked individually. Additionally, it makes the review of actions pursued easier to review by the agency. Furthermore, the response to the Form 483 should contain sufficient granularity so the agency understand the steps being pursued to correct the non-compliances. For example, in responding to the Form 483, the doctor recommends the following information should be considered in the response:

1. A restatement of the Form 483 Observation;

2. The proposed corrective action or plan (ensure past, current, and future states influenced by the observation are assessed);

3. Reference to the specific CAPA number;

4. Ensure root cause is determined and addressed;

5. Potential impact to product;

6. Potential impact to the quality system; and

7. The targeted date for completion.

Finally, please do not forget to add a cover letter to the response. Remember, a thorough and well-thought response to a From 483 is an organization's best preemptive defense in preventing the issuance of a warning letter. One final thought, make sure all of the corrections are implemented and effective. Why? Because during the agency's next friendly visit to your facility, they will revisit previous observations and verify they are closed.

Disagreeing with an Observation

It is ok to disagree with a Form 483 observation; however, it is up to the offending organization to draft a salient response that delineates the points of disagreement. If an organization disagrees, it is incumbent upon the organization to provide supporting evidence as to why they believe the observation has been incorrectly made. The agency's expectation is that these types of disputes can be resolved as part of the inspection debrief; however, that is not always the case. One final thought, never ever, ever, ever, ever, inform the agency that the reason your organization cannot achieve compliance is because of resources constraints. As Dr. D has stated on multiple occasions, "Compliance to regulations is just part of the price of admission to play in the medical device industry." If an organization does not have or will not invest in adequate resources, they are playing in the wrong sandbox.

226

Takeaways from Chapter 21

At the end of the day, there are two options in regards to Form 483s. For option one, an organization can be proactive, accept the Form 483, and treat is as an opportunity for pursuing continuous improvement, while driving compliance to the QSR. For option two, an organization can ignore the Form 483. In doing so, said organization should be prepared to deal with the proverbial opening of a can of FDA "whoop-ass" and the subsequent warning letter that will be issued.

Chapter 22 – Responding to an FDA Warning Letter

Responding to a Warning Letter

So your organization has received a warning letter from the FDA – now what? For starters, the agency has quickly upped the ante in regards to taking the next steps in ensuring your organization clearly understands that a continued state of non-compliance is not acceptable. According to Margaret A. Hamburg, M.D. (Commissioner of the FDA), in a comment made during the August 6th, 2009 FDLI Conference, "FDA's enforcement arm is back in business." In short, the message sent was short and sweet. Violations of the Act are going to result in a strong enforcement response from the agency. The FDA issues warning letters when; (a) Form 483 responses are seriously deficient; (b) an organization has failed to respond to a Form 483, or (c) the violations of the Act are so egregious, the FDA has decided to move rapidly to warning letter. In fact, the warning letter signifies the beginning of some serious regulatory hurt being unleashed by the FDA. Dr. D likes to call this FDA Purgatory. Once an organization migrates to under the umbrella of an FDA warning letter, an immediate impact to their business is quickly realized. The agency is no longer obliged to review and approve new product submissions. Can you say no PMA approvals? Additionally, letters needed by foreign governments for product exportation, a.k.a., FDA Export Certificates are no longer reviewed, approved, and signed. For medical device manufacturers these certificates are formally known as: (a) Certificate to Foreign Government; and (b) Certificate of Exportability. The impact to an organization's bottom line can be severe, as these certificates begin to expire. The amount of time spent in warning-letter land is entirely up to the organization and the number of objectionable conditions noted in the warning letter. If the responses formulated and sent to the agency lack depth and detail, and the

FDA believes the responses are inadequate or ineffective, the time spent in the proverbial "land of lost opportunities" can be years. Dr. D strongly recommends the pulling out of all stops so organizations can quickly extricate themselves from FDA Purgatory.

What is a Warning Letter?

Just because an organization is a Form 483 recipient, at the close of an inspection, does not necessarily translate into a warning letter. Upon conclusion of an inspection, the FDA investigator is tasked with writing the Establishment Inspection Report (EIR). The completed EIR will be reviewed at the local district office; and if the reviewer believes the content and evidence depicted in the EIR points to serious deficiencies in an establishment's quality system, then a warning letter will be issued. Additionally, as of April of 2009, the agency has adopted a policy of automatically issuing warning letters to establishments failing to respond to a Form 483 within the allotted 15-days. Ouch! There will be no susurrus (look-it-up) opening phrases in the initial paragraph of the FDA's warning letter. In fact, the warning letter's opening paragraph typically commences with, *"During an inspection of your firm"* and ends with *"Please notify this office in writing within fifteen (15) working days from the date you receive this letter of the specific steps you have taken to correct the noted violations, including an explanation of how you plan to prevent these violations, or similar violations, from occurring again. Include documentation of the corrective action you have taken."*

According to the FDA, the issuance of a warning letter is one of the tools in their FDA enforcement bag. The primary purpose of the warning letter is to attempt to extract a voluntary correction of objectionable conditions by the agency. Remember, the issuance of a warning letter is not the final regulatory action available to the agency. In fact, Dr. D's position is the warning letter is the proverbial warning shot. As the doctor stated in the opening paragraph, the warning letter results in a significant interruptions in the day-to-day activities of the recipients.

What Happens When a Warning Letter is Received?

The good news is that the US Marshalls have not shown up at your establishment's doorstep to chain and padlock the doors. More good news - a warning letter, although painful, is a recoverable event and can make an organization stronger. How does the saying go, "What doesn't kill you makes you stronger!" Dr. D strongly recommends that if the organization does not have the expertise to respond to the warning letter or does not retain legal counsel that understands the entire process, this expertise be acquired immediately. There are many consultant firms that specialize in the assisting establishments in extracting themselves from FDA Purgatory. One thing an organization must remember is that the warning letter is not a simple overnight fix. Warning letters typically result in a protracted period where corrections to the objectionable conditions are achieved. This is not rocket science folks, the more observations depicted in the warning letter, the longer the stay in FDA Purgatory. In penning the book Devine Guidance, the doctor has reviewed hundreds of warning letters awarded to device manufacturers. In one case, an offender received a warning letter with 19 observations (reference next section). Dr. D will probably be retired before this establishment finds itself back in the good graces of the agency.

Sample Warning Letter

On multiple occasions throughout 2010, the doctor has made multiple references back to a device manufacturer that was on the receiving end of a 19-observation warning letter. For those readers that have never had a chance to truly appreciate the power of the agency and their resolve to enforce compliance with the Act, this is an excellent example of a warning letter. Obviously, the device manufacturer was not happy with their award; however, compliance to the QSR is only a small piece of the price of admission into the medical device industry. One final note: Dr. D has taken the liberty to redact the organization's name and the name of their CEO

WARNING LETTER

CMS # 89144

March 25, 2010

Dr. Redacted, CEO and Chairman
Redacted Med Devices, Inc.
7402 York Road #100
Towson, MD 21204-7532

Dear Dr. Redacted:

During an inspection of your firm located in Towson, Maryland on September 28, 2009, through November 6, 2009, an investigator from the United States Food and Drug Administration (FDA) determined that your firm manufactures electrogastrogram (EGG) devices. Under section 201(h) of the Federal Food, Drug, and Cosmetic Act (the Act), 21 U.S.C. 321 (h), these products are devices because they are intended for use in the diagnosis of disease or other conditions or in the cure, mitigation, treatment, or prevention of disease, or are intended to affect the structure or function of the body.

This inspection revealed that these devices are adulterated within the meaning of section 501(h) Act (21 U.S.C. 351 (h)), in that the methods used in, or the facilities or controls used for, their manufacture, packing, storage, or installation are not in conformity with the Current Good Manufacturing Practice (CGMP) requirements of the Quality System (QS) regulation found at Title 21, Code of Federal Regulations (C.F.R.), Part 820. These violations include, but are not limited to, the following:

1. Failure to establish and maintain adequate procedures to ensure that the design requirements relating to a device are appropriate and address the intended use of the device, including the needs of the user and patient, as required by 21 CFR 820.30(c). For example procedures for Version (b)(4) EGG machine in (b)(4) or for the upgrade made to the Research Version device in (b)(4) which included a new Research Waterload Version and a Waterload Version.

2. Failure to establish and maintain adequate procedures for defining and documenting design output in terms that allow an adequate evaluation of conformance to design input requirements, as required by 21 CFR 820.30(d). For example:

> *a. When requested, design output procedures and/or requirements for the upgrade from Version (b)(4) to Version (b)(4) done by (b)(4) and for the upgrade from Version (b)(4) Research device to Versions (b)(4) Research, Research Waterload device done (b)(4) could not be provided.*
> *b. When requested, no evidence that design outputs were established and evaluated against design inputs document (b)(4) was provided.*
> *c. There is no record of review and approval of device labeling, including review and approval of the labeling for the Research Version (b)(4) released (b)(4)*

3. Failure to establish and maintain adequate procedures to ensure that formal documented reviews of the design results are planned and conducted at appropriate stages of the device's design development, as required by 21 CFR 820.30(e). For example, procedures were not established to ensure formal documented reviews of the design during the design planning process.

4. Failure to establish and maintain adequate procedures for verifying the device design and documenting the results of the design verification, including identification of the design, method(s), the date, and the individual(s) performing the verification, as required by 21 CFR820.30(t). For example:

> *a. When requested, no documentation to confirm that the finished product conformed to specified requirement as stated in the (b)(4) was provided.*
> *b. The design plan identifies what testing will be done to ensure general assembly requirements are met; however, when requested, the documentation to support testing that was performed on the following activities could not be located: (1) 'Test Type CF EGG Lead on CWE Head Stage," (2) "Test Type B on Respiration Connection" and (3) "Verify Cart - Tip Test."*

5. Failure to establish and maintain adequate procedures for validating the device design, as required by 21 CFR 820.30(g). For example:

> *a. When requested no evidence to show that the validation test was performed as stated in Test Report (b)(4) was provided.*
> *b. When requested, no evidence to support that the finished device was validated to include validation with the EGGSAS software was provided.*
> *c. The Failure Modes Effect Analysis FMEA described in (b)(4) does not define the Average Likelihood of Occurrence (ALOO) for each value.*

6. Failure to establish and maintain procedures for the identification, documentation, validation or where appropriate verification, review, and approval of design changes before their implementation, as required by 21 CFR 820.30(i). For example:

> *a. When requested, no procedure identifying how design changes made to the device are processed was provided.*
> *b. When requested, no evidence that the changes made to the finished device or the research, research waterload, or waterload software versions were verified or*

validated to ensure that the changes are effective and did not adversely affect the finished product was provided.

c. When requested, no evidence to support the device software update from Research Version (b)(4) to Version (b)(4) was verified to meet design requirements as stated in the (b)(4) was provided.

d. When requested, no documentation to support that the changes to EGGSAS software were verified to demonstrate the functionality was provided. The EGGSAS version (b)(4) software is the software component for the EGG machine that is used in conjunction with the (b)(4) to provide a diagnosis of gastric motility disorders.

7. Failure to document all activities required under 21 CFR 820.100, Corrective and Preventive 21 CFR 820.100(b). For example:

a. Email correspondence between the dates of November 26, 2008 and December 1, 2008 discuss an install program for the Redacted Med Devices companion program, known as the Reader, and problems encountered during testing. The test methods are not identified, and the software used to test the program is not identified. The final email correspondence refers to a "problem" identified in the folder the program is run on. The program is not identified, nor is a resolution documented.

b. Email correspondence dated December 2, 2008 discuss the Redacted Med Devices companion programs known as the Reader and (b)(4) programs corrupting the EGGSAS software making the EGGSAS software "disappear" when the (b)(4) program was uninstalled. The emails discuss testing the Reader and (b)(4) programs to ensure the problem was fixed; however, no resolution is identified and/or documented.

c. Email correspondence between the dates of February 1 and February 3, 2009 discuss changes, upgrades, procedure/policy and software testing; however, the results of the testing or test methods are not documented.

d. Email correspondence on May 18 and 19, 2009 discuss the uninstall of EGGSAS software version (b)(4) on a Windows 98 notebook, which resulted in the uninstall of other programs on the customer's computer (not related to Redacted Med Devices). In an email from Mr. M. Ted Braid (CIO, Redacted Med Devices), he stated support is not offered for older versions of the EGGSAS software; however, an exception would be made in this instance. The email ended with the offer to purchase new equipment to support the older version of software or to purchase the newer version of software. The email was closed, and no date is provided. There is no evidence of an investigation.

8. Failure to establish and maintain procedures that address the identification, documentation, evaluation, segregation, and disposition of nonconforming product, as required by 21 CFR 820.90(a). For example, there is no defined method of identifying, documenting and evaluating nonconforming product and any investigation associated with the nonconforming product. Specifically, email correspondence between the dates of June 29 and July 6, 2009, indicate the need to correct a problem with the data entry field on the waterload software version; however, no further documentation is available addressing this issue.

9. Failure to validate computer software for its intended use according to an established protocol when computers or automated data processing systems are used as part of production or the quality system, as required by 21 CFR 820.70(i). For example, when requested no validation documentation to support the commercial off-the-shelf program (b)(4) used to capture complaints, returned merchandise and service requests was provided.

10. Failure to establish and maintain adequate acceptance procedures, where appropriate, to ensure that specified requirements for in-process product and finished device acceptance are met as required by 21 CFR 820.80(c) and (d). Finished device acceptance includes ensuring that each product, run, lot, or batch of finished devices meets acceptance criteria. For example, electrogastrogram machine components and finished product acceptance and/or rejection criteria have not been established.

11. Failure to establish and maintain procedures for identifying product during all stages of receipt, production, distribution, and installation to prevent mixups, as required by 21 CFR 820.60. For example, there is no procedure or mechanism for identifying individual equipment components, software, or finished device. Specifically, there are three versions of the EGGSAS software all identified as Version (b)(4): (1) a waterload version; (2) a research - waterload version; and (3) a research version.

12. Failure to establish and maintain procedures for control and distribution of finished devices to ensure that only those devices approved for release are distributed and to maintain distribution records which include or refer to the location of (1) the name and address of the initial consignee; (2) the identification and quantity of devices shipped; (3) the date shipped; and (4) any control number(s) used, as required by 21 CFR 820.160. For example, when requested, procedures for controlling and distributing finished devices and distribution records for products released into distribution for 2008 and 2009 were not provided.

13. Failure to establish and maintain device master records (DMR's), as required by 21 CFR 820.181. For example, when requested, no DMR for the EGGSAS software used in the three Redacted Med Devices Electrogastrogram versions: Research, Research Waterload, and Waterload was provided.

14. Failure to maintain adequate device master records that include, or refer to the location of, device specifications including appropriate drawings, composition, formulation, component specifications, and software specifications, as required by 21 CFR 820.181(a). For example, when requested, the software specifications for the software update that occurred in (b)(4) or the software updates that occurred between (b)(4) could not be located.

15. Failure to establish and maintain procedures to ensure that device history records (DHR) for each batch, lot, or unit are maintained to demonstrate that the device is manufactured in accordance with the device master record and the requirements of 21 CFR Part 820, as required by 21 CFR 810.184. For example:

> *a. When requested, no DHR for the research, research-waterload or the waterload software Version (b)(4) tested and distributed to customers was provided.*
> *b. There is no record of device labeling.*
> *c. Changes to the software are not documented in the Design History File and are not tracked and/or verified. There is no documentation listing the number and/or type of changes that were made.*

16. Failure to establish and maintain procedures to control all documents that are required by 21 CFR Part 820, as required by 21 CFR 820.40. The procedures should designate an individual(s) to review for adequacy and approve prior to issuance all documents established to meet the requirements of 21 CFR Part 820. For example:

a. When requested, no procedures which address document control were provided.
b. The following unapproved documents are maintained in the Device History File, stored electronically, or are contract/(b)(4) agreements:

1. The Redacted Med Devices Company, Inc. (b)(4) with no review or approval signatures.
2. The Design Plan entitled (b)(4) undated with no review or approval signatures.
3. SOP number (b)(4) no approval signature.
4. Document number (b)(4) undated with no approval signature.
5. Document number (b)(4) dated Ma 14, 2003 with no approval signature.
6. Test Report (b)(4) written by the firm's independent consultant, but not approved by Redacted Med Devices management
7. (b)(4) but does not have a review or approval signature.
8. (b)(4) but does not have a review or approval signature.
9. (b)(4) but does not have a review or approval signature.
10. (b)(4) undated with no approval signature
11. (b)(4) undated with no approval signature
12. (b)(4) undated with no approval signature
13. (b)(4) but updated.
14. "CONTRACT SERVICES AGREEMENT" between Redacted Med Devices Company, Inc (b)(4) undated with no signatures.

17. Failure of management with executive responsibility to review the suitability and effectiveness of the quality system at defined intervals and with sufficient frequency according to established of 21 CFR Part 820 and the manufacturer's established quality policy and objectives, as required by 21 CFR 820.20(c). For example, when requested no documentation to support management reviews are conducted was provided.

18. Failure to establish procedures for quality audits and conduct such audits to assure that the quality system is in compliance with the established quality system requirements and to determine the effectiveness of the quality system, as required by 21 CFR 820.22. For example, when requested, procedures for quality audits were not provided. Quality audits have not been conducted since 2003.

19. Failure to establish procedures for identifying training needs and ensure that all personnel are trained to adequately perform their assigned responsibilities, as required by 21 CFR 820.25(b). For example, when requested, documentation that training was performed according to the design plan for the upgraded device from Version (b)(4) to Version (b)(4) could not be located. A troubleshooting chart was scheduled to be created; however, it could not be located; and training materials and a training class were to be provided/conducted on Customer Service and Sales/Marketing according to the Design Plan; however, the training materials or documentation that the training was conducted could not be located.

Our inspection also revealed that your electrogastrogram devices are misbranded under section 502(t)(2) of the Act, 21 U.S.C. 352(t)(2), in that your firm failed or refused to furnish material or information respecting the device that is required by or under section 519 of the Act, 21 U.S.C. 360i, and 21 C.F.R. Part 803 Medical Device Reporting (MDR) regulation. Significant deviations include, but are not limited to, the following:

Failure or refusal to furnish material or information respecting the device that is required by or under section 519 of the Act, 21 U.S.C. 360i, and 21 CFR 803 - Medical Device Reporting

(MDR) regulation. For example, when requested procedures for MDR reportable events were not provided.

You should take prompt action to correct the violations addressed in this letter. Failure to promptly correct these violations may result in regulatory action being initiated by the Food and Drug Administration without further notice. These actions include, but are not limited to, seizure, injunction, and/or civil money penalties. Also, federal agencies are advised of the issuance of all Warning Letters about devices so that they may take this information into account when considering the award of contracts. Additionally, premarket approval applications for Class III devices to which the Quality System regulation deviations are reasonably related will not be approved until the violations have been corrected. Requests for Certificates to Foreign Governments will not be granted until the violations related to the subject devices have been corrected.

Please notify this office in writing within fifteen (15) working days from the date you receive this letter of the specific steps you have taken to correct the noted violations, including an explanation of how you plan to prevent these violations, or similar violations, from occurring again. Include documentation of the corrective action you have taken. If your planned corrections will occur over time, please include a timetable for implementation of those corrections. If corrective action cannot be completed within 15 working days, state the reason for the delay and the time within which the corrections will be completed.

Finally, you should know that this letter is not intended to be an all-inclusive list of the violations at your facility. It is your responsibility to ensure compliance with applicable laws and regulations administered by FDA. The specific violations noted in this letter and in the Inspectional Observations, Form FDA 483 (FDA 483), issued at the close out of the inspection may be symptomatic of serious problems in your firm's manufacturing and quality assurance systems. You should investigate and determine the causes of the violations, and take prompt actions to correct the violations and to bring your products into compliance.

Please send your reply to the U.S. Food and Drug Administration, Attention: Anne Aberdeen, Compliance Officer, 6000 Metro Drive, Suite 101, Baltimore, MD 21215. If you have questions regarding any issues in this letter, please contact Ms. Aberdeen at (410) 779-5134.

Sincerely,

/s/

Evelyn Bonnin
District Director
Baltimore District

How to Respond to a Warning Letter

Responding to a warning letter is similar to that of a Form 483. Upon receipt of

the warning letter, an organization has 15-working days to respond to the FDA.

Additionally, the doctor strongly recommends that legal counsel review all correspondence with the agency. Once again, the recipient of the warning letter should draft a cover letter with all correspondences back to the agency. There will be several during the life of the warning letter so meticulous records of each submission should be kept. For example, in responding to the warning letter, the doctor recommends the following information should be considered in the response:

8. A restatement of the Form 483 Observation;

9. The proposed corrective action or plan (ensure past, current, and future states influenced by the observation are assessed);

10. Reference to the specific CAPA number;

11. Ensure root cause is determined and addressed;

12. Potential impact to product;

13. Potential impact to the quality system; and

14. The targeted date for completion.

Warning Letter Watch outs – What Not to Do

Dr. D has a few watch outs he will share with the readers.

1. Never, never, never, never, complain the FDA has singled out your company and is intentionally picking on you. The argument will never fly.

2. Never fail to respond back to the agency, within the 15-days allotted or committed dates made by your organization as part of the correction activities.

3. Dr. D strongly dissuades pursuing the Utah Medical approach, arguing the law. Why? The FDA is the keeper of the law, which is why most arguments are futile.

4. Remember, the agency will verify objectionable conditions have been closed prior to lifting the warning letter, so ensure all correction activities are closed prior to

scheduling a follow-up visit by the agency.

5. Always provide the agency with sufficient detail and supporting documentation that reflects the actions pursued in support of the corrections.

6. If the corrections are going to take a significant amount of time, give the FDA reasonable timetable for correcting all of the objectionable conditions. Ensure that status updates are routinely provided to the agency.

7. Never downplay or minimize the seriousness of the observation. Remember, the FDA would not have issued the warning letter if they did not believe the enforcement action was warranted,

Takeaways from Chapter 22

Yes, warning letters are life-changing events for device manufacturers; however, they are recoverable. Dr. D always recommends getting legal counsel and industry experts involved when responding to a warning letter, reviewing subsequent correspondences to the agency, and the actual steps pursued in correction the objectionable conditions. Always remember, the FDA is not picking on you but they have a responsibility to protect public health. It is the agency's position that the objectionable conditions delineated within each waning letter could have an adverse effect on public health.

Chapter 23 – Consent Decree "Now What?"

Consent Decree – Now What?

Once the agency has decided to progress to consent decree, all bets are off because now, the courts are involved. By now, your organization has probably endeared themselves with the agency by an overall lack of understanding of the Food, Drug, and Cosmetic Act, the Quality System Regulation (QSR), and the overall authority granted the agency under the Act. As Dr. D has stated time-and-time-again, failure to comply is not an option. Compliance to the Act and the QSR is mandated by law. Guess what? It is the FDA that decides if an organization is compliant with the law, through the process of establishment inspections. By moving the issue of continued lack of compliance into the Federal Courts, the agency has exhausted all avenues previously afforded. Remember there is no single event or series of events that propels the agency to pursue a consent decree. For example, the offending establishment probably received a Form 483. For example, the offending establishment has product that was hurting patients (a.k.a., not safe and effective). For example, the offending establishment probably received a warning letter. For example, the offending establishment has not been responsive to the FDA, e.g., failing to respond to a request within 15-days. At this juncture, the FDA probably believes the offending establishment just does not comprehend the ongoing messages being sent by the agency. The end-result of any of the previously mentioned examples or combination of these examples can result in a consent decree. People, this is not good, what part of compliance is not being understood? In fact, if Dr. D ran the agency, the first thing I would recommend, once an organization moved to operating under a consent decree, is the measuring of the Chief Jailable Officer (CJO) for that infamous orange jumpsuit. In fact, I would institute orange-jumpsuit Fridays for all of the offending establishment's officers just to drive home the point of mandated compliance.

Remember, consent decree and the resulting actions are now being driven by the courts

and all bets are off in regards to when normal business operations will return, if ever.

What is Consent Decree?

A consent decree is a legal agreement between the FDA and the offending

establishment that will be the blueprint to drive the required changes to systems,

procedures, and behaviors needed to bring the offending organization back into

compliance. One of the objectives of the consent decree is to prevent protracted litigation

within the courts. Once the terms of the consent decree are agreed upon between the

agency and the offending establishment, the agreement is signed by the establishment's

chief officer (preferable the CEO), a US Attorney, and the judge presiding over the

matter in the applicable US District Court. Once signed, the consent decree is forwarded

to the FDA, issued to the offending establishment, and the real work, correcting the

objectionable conditions commences. Since the establishment has failed miserably in

their attempts to attain compliance, a third-party consultant is brought into the mix to

assist in correcting the objectionable conditions. Can you say expensive? Dr. D can hear

the controller screaming as the dollars begin flying out the door faster than F-22 Raptor

in full afterburner. Additionally, if the offending establishment, about to enter the consent

decree process, has not retained outside counsel, now would be the time. Furthermore, if

the offending establishment thinks the third-party consultants are expensive, just wait

until the payment of the fines being levied is required, for not fulfilling the terms of the

agreement quickly or for plain old-fashion punitive purposes. Finally, if the added

expense of consultants and the payment of fines do not get the organization's attention, how about a forced market withdraws, product seizures, or delays in new product approvals. Can you say a significant interruption of revenue streams?

Remember the agency, if necessary, will employ the courts to prevent establishments from placing or introducing product into commerce, especially if products are causing injury or death; or an establishment's continued lack of compliance with the Act. Can you say product seizures? As with all regulatory actions pursued by the agency, they will ask "in writing" for an establishment to withdraw product voluntarily. Then it is back to the courts, if the requests are ignored or declined. Dr. D is not sure why any organization, being managed by sane and rational management, would ever refuse an agency request. Failure to comply with an agency request, while operating under a consent decree, can be equated to severe pain being unleashed by the agency. Trust Dr. D when I say, "the CJO will sleep better at night when compliance is the norm and not the exception."

Final Thoughts

For starters, establishments entering into a consent decree will not be extricating themselves from this environment quickly. In fact, consent decrees could take several years of hard work to bring offending establishments back into compliance with the Act. To give you an idea of how expensive a consent decree can be, Schering-Plough (consent decree – 2002) was initially fined $500M dollars. If that figure does not get your attention, how about the estimated $1B Abbot Laboratories (consent decree – 1999) spent correcting objectionable conditions while living in the land of consent decree. The best advice Dr. D can give device manufacturers is never enter the realm of consent decree. Yes – device manufacturers will receive an occasional Form 483, because systems are managed by people, and people make mistakes. However, Form 483 observations need to be taken seriously and corrections to objectionable conditions quickly made. Yes – some device manufacturers will receive waning letters. Once these letters are received, it is incumbent upon the recipients to draw up a detailed plan for correction and work closely with the agency in correcting the objectionable conditions. Once an offending establishment moves ongoing operations under a consent decree, all bets are off and the expensive fun stuff commences. In this pay me now pay me later scenario, it is a wise investment: (a) to pay for the development and implementation of a robust manufacturing environment; (b) that is compliant with all aspects of the Act; and (c) capable of sustaining a compliant environment with adequate staffing resources; than to dance with the agency in US District Court. Why? Because $1B can buy a whole lot of R & D versus paying for remediation programs.

Takeaways from Chapter 23

There is just one message that needs to be taken away from this chapter. That message is, "consent decrees are expensive." If the process of paying the third-party consultants does not grab the attention of the controller, rest assured the fines levied by the courts should. One final thought, with no new product approvals coming from the FDA on the horizon, your competitors will be thanking you as your customer base and market share quickly begin to erode. Couple the eroding market share with the agency's unwillingness to sign Certificates for Exportation and the potential for financial Armageddon begins to unfold.

References

References

AAMI – Association for the Advancement of Medical Instrumentation Website. (2010, June). *AAMI homepage.* Retrieved June 24, 2010, from http://www.aami.org/about/index.html

Aczel, D., & Sounderpandian, J. (2006). *Complete business statistics* (6th ed.). Boston: McGraw-Hill Irwin.

Anatomy of a consent decree. (2007, April). Eye on the FDA. Retrieved December 13, 2010, from http://www.eyeonfda.com

Appel, C. (2010). *How to respond to and avoid FDA form 483s.* Retrieved November 27, 2010, from http://www.veriteq.com

Bangert, M. (2008, September). The fundamentals of data collection. *Quality 47*(9).

Buffaloe, V. (2006). Outsourcing and the quality system. *Biomedical Engineering & Technology, 40*(4). Retrieved January 4, 2007, from http://proquest.umi.com

Burd, M. & Chrai, S. (2004, June). *After the consent decree – a uphill battle for affected companies.* Retrieved December 16, 2010, from http://biopharminternational.findpharma.com

Chase, N. (1999, October). Reports standardize receiving inspection. *Quality, 38*(6).

Code of Federal Regulation. (2010, April). *Title 21 Part 803: Medical device reporting.* Washington, D.C.: U. S. Government Printing Office.

Code of Federal Regulation. (2010, April). *Title 21 Part 820: Quality system regulation.* Washington, D.C.: U. S. Government Printing Office.

Cognizant Technology Solutions. (2001). CFR Part 11 Compliance – The cognizant Approach. Retrieved July 13, 2010, from http://www.21cfrpart11.com/files/library/compliance/cfr_whitepaper.pdf

Cooper, R. & Fleder, J. (2005). *Responding* to a form 483 or warning letter: A practical guide. *Food and Drug Law Journal, 60*(4).

Chesney, D. & Kelley, A. (1998, December). *Responding to 483s and warning letters.* ISPE Boston Chapter Website. Retrieved December 8, 2010, from http://www.ispeboston.org/technical_articles

Davis, A. (2010, November). *How to respond to FDA 483.* Retrieved November 27, 2010, from http://www.ehow.com

Devine. C. (2009, July). *Exploring the effectiveness of defensive-receiving inspection for medical device manufacturers: a mixed method study.* Published doctoral dissertation. Northcentral University. Prescott Valley, AZ.

Dimensioning and tolerancing. (1994). *American Society of Mechanical Engineers ASME Y14.5M-1994.* New York, NY.

Dodge, H. (1955). Skip-lot sampling plan. *Industrial Quality Control, 11*(5).

EN 980:2008. (2010, May). *Symbols for use in the labeling of medical devices.* European Standard – Prepared by: Technical Committee CEN/CLC/TC 3.

EN ISO 11607-1:2009. (2010, March). *Packaging for terminally sterilized medical devices – Part 1: Requirements for materials, sterile barrier systems and packaging systems.* International Organization for Standardization.

EN ISO 11607-2:2006. (2006, July). *Packaging for terminally sterilized medical devices – Part 2: Validation requirements for forming, sealing, and assembly processes.* International Organization for Standardization.

EN ISO 17025 (2005, May). *General requirements for the competence of testing and calibration laboratories-ISO/IEC 17025: 2005.* Retrieved July 23, 2010, from http://ihs.store/spectstore

Ericson, J. (2006, November). Lean inspection through supplier partnership. *Quality Progress, 39*(11), 36-41.

FDA - U.S. Food and Drug Administration Website. (2010). Warning letters. Retrieved http://www.fda.gov/ICECI/EnforcementActions/WarningLetters/

Fink, R., & Margavio, T. (1994). Economic models for single sample acceptance sampling plans, no inspection, and 100 percent inspection. *Decision Sciences, 25*(4).

Foster, M. (2003, August). 3-D and G D & T takes a concept to production. *Quality, 42*(8). Retrieved November 3, 2008, from http://proquest.umi.com

Foxton, J. (1996). Negotiating quality through customer communications. *Managing Service Quality, 6*(5). Retrieved November 5, 2008, from http://proquest.umi.com

Freiesleben, J. (2006). Costs and benefits of inspection systems and optimal allocation for uniform defect propensity. *The International Journal of Quality & Reliability, 23*(5). Retrieved January 24, 2007, from http://proquest.umi.com

Garvey, J. (2010, January). *FDA form 483 & warning letter response & planning.* Compliance Architects Website. Retrieved December 8, 2010, from http://www.compliancearchitects.com

Ghinato, P. (1998, August). Quality control methods: towards modern approaches through well-established principles. *Total Quality Management, 9*(6).

GHTF/SG3/N99-10:2004. (2004, January). *Quality management systems-process validation guidance.* Global Harmonization Task Force. Retrieved July 26, from http://www.ghtf.org/documents/sg3/sg3_fd_n99-10_edition2.pdf

Godshalk, J. (2009). *Best practices: Responding to FDA form 483.* Retrieved November, 27, 2010, from http://fdanews.com/ext/conference

ISTA-Procedure 2A:2008. (2008). *Packaged-products weighing 150 lb (68 kg) or less.* International Safe Transit Association.

Juran, J. & Godfrey, A. (1998). *Juran's quality handbook* (5th ed.). New York, New York: McGraw-Hill.

Kanter, J. (2008, June). Audits crucial to supplier wellbeing. *Supply Management, 13*(12). Retrieved November 13, 2008, from http://proquest.umi.com

Kappele, W., & Raffaldi, J. (2006, June). Gage R & R improves quality and profitability. *Quality, 45*(6). Retrieved October 31, 2008, from http://proquest.umi.com

Lookabaugh, M. (2006, May). *Responding to FDA 483s and warning letters – presentation to Parenteral Drug Association.* Parexel Consulting. Lowell, MA.

Mayer, K. J., Nickerson, J. A., & Owan, H. (2004, August). *Are* supply and plant inspections complements or substitutes – a strategic and operational assessment of inspection practices in biotechnology. *Management Science, 50*(8).

Medical Device Directive. (1993). Council Directive 93/42/EEC. *Medical Device Safety Service.* Retrieved January 11, 2010, from http://directive93-42-eec.htm

Medical devices – quality management systems – requirements for regulatory purposes. (2007). EN ISO 13485:2003/AC:2007.

Mehta, M., & Kauffman, P. (2006, August). Improve Gage R & R results. *Six Sigma Forum Magazine, 5*(4). Retrieved October 31, 2008, from http://proquest.umi.com

Merriam-Webster's On-Line Dictionary. (2010). *Statistics definition.* Retrieved November 25, 2010, from http://www.merriam-webster.com/dictionary/statistics

Morris, R. (2007, July). Enhance first article inspection. *Quality, 46*(7).

Nelson, C. (2010, May). *The definition of FDA 483*. Retrieved November 27, 2010, from
http://www.ehow.com

Poor supplier control causing recalls, FDA says; contract is key to success. (2007, May).
The Sheet – Medical Device Quality Control, 11(6). Danvers, MA.

Prop 65 News. (2010, June). *Your online guide to California's unique environmental
statute, proposition 65*. Retrieved June 21, 2010, from
http://www.prop65news.com/pubs/brochure/madesimple.html

Sampling procedures and tables for inspection by attributes. (2003). *American Society for
Quality ANSI/ASQ Z1.4-2003*. Milwaukee, WI.

Sampling procedures and tables for inspection by variables. (2008). *American Society for
Quality ANSI/ASQ Z1.9-2008*. Milwaukee, WI.

Schildhouse, J. (2005, summer). An interview with Sarmento Silva. *Journal of Supply
Chain Management, 41*(3). Retrieved November 4, 2008, from
http://proquest.umi.com

Slobodow, B., Abdullah, O., & Babuschak, C. (2008). When supplier partnerships aren't.
MIT Sloan Management Review, 49(2).

Sutton, S. (2006, September). *Counting Colonies*. The Microbiology Network. Retrieved
July 4, 2010, From http://www.microbiol.org/white.papers/WP.count.colony.htm

Sutton, S. (2009, August). *Qualification of an environmental monitoring program –
selection and justification of sampling sites*. Pharmaceutical Microbiology Forum
Newsletter, 14(8), Retrieved July 4, 2010, from http://www.microbiologyforum
.Org/PMFNews/PMFNews.14.08.0808.pdf

Taylor, N. (2009, February). *Ignore a form 483? Not wise say FDA*. Retrieved November
27, 2010, from http://www.in-pharmatechnologist.com

Taylor, W. (1993, November). Classifying defects and selecting AQLs. *FDC Control,
Food Drug & Cosmetic Division ASQC, 103*. Retrieved March 23, 2007, from
http://www.variation.com/techlib/as-1.html

Taylor, W. (1996). Selecting statistically valid sampling plans. *Quality Engineering,
10*(2). Retrieved March 5, 2007, from http://www.variation.com/techlib/as-7.html

Tierney, P., Burke, R., O'Donnell, B., & McAteer, J. (2010, May). *Environmental monitoring – maintaining a clean room.* Pharm Pro Magazine. Retrieved July 5, 2010, from http://www.pharmpro.com/articles/2010/06/ clean-rooms-Environmental-Monitoring-Maintaining-a-Clean-Room/

Vijayaraghavan, R. (2000, September). Design and evaluation of skip-lot sampling plans of type SkSP-3. *Journal of Applied Statistics, 27*(7).

Zhang, Z. (2008, June). Literature review of purchasing management in service industry. *Management Science and Engineering, 2*(2).

Zhenjia, Z. (2008, June). Literature review of purchasing management in service industry. *Management Science and Engineering 2*(2).

CPSIA information can be obtained at www.ICGtesting.com
Printed in the USA
LVOW09s1530190913

353228LV00011B/458/P

9 781466 358768